FINANCING EDUCATION: ISSUES AND ANSWERS

Donald C. Shields

University of Cincinnati


John F. Cragan

University of Wisconsin — Superior

Copyright 1972

by Donald C. Shields and John F. Cragan

All Rights Reserved. L.C. Number 72-85456

International Standard Book Number 0-913036-03-X

Campus Press ● P.O. Box 4261 ● Minneapolis ● 55414

# PREFACE

This book provides an introduction to the issues and arguments underlying the question, "What should be the policy toward financing elementary and secondary education in the United States?" The specific analysis focuses on the proposition, "That governmental financial support for all public elementary and secondary education in the United States should be provided exclusively by the federal government." The "Issue Blocks" appearing in Chapter Five present in our judgement a solid introduction to the central concerns of this subject. The analysis of the proposition appearing in Chapter Two should both enable a clear grasp of the extensiveness of this topic and provide insight into the criteria utilized for inclusion of material in the issue blocks.

We have tried to make FINANCING EDUCATION: ISSUES AND ANSWERS both practical and theoretical. Practical in the sense that we have developed the major affirmative and negative issues through extensive topic analysis and by combining argument and evidence into a usable form. Theoretical in the sense that we have tried to present a concise treatment of current debate theory and practice. The achievement of both objectives is a delicate balance. Many may conclude that we have failed. Nevertheless, we believe it a worthy goal to attempt topic analysis along with the presentation of theoretical material that can serve as a refresher to the experienced debater or function as a teacher aid in training the novice debater or classroom student.

To meet these dual goals several new features have been included. One new feature, Coaches 'Corner', deserves particular mention because it provides an opportunity for you to interact with the thoughts of other coaches regarding contemporary debate practices. Responses and critical input on areas of particular interest are welcomed. Manuscripts may be sent to the authors in care of Campus Press.

Finally, we wish to express our appreciation to Lee Cotugno and Art Carter for their criticism and assistance in preparing this manuscript. They had primary responsiblity for Chapters One, Five and Six. Their help has proven to be invaluable.

D. C. S.<br>
J. F. C.

Minneapolis
April 22, 1972

# TABLE OF CONTENTS

**Preface**                                                                                                    **Page**

**Chapter**

# CHAPTER ONE

## AN OVERVIEW OF THE TOPIC

### Lee Cotugno and Art Carter*

Concern over the nation's public elementary and secondary schools has been particularily pronounced of late. Public attention and discussion has been generated by an increasing awareness and virtual "crises of confidence" in the ability of government to achieve its objectives at all levels. In this sense part of the perception of the problem of the nation's schools is related to the problems of American society at large. Current school operation and educational policy is under attack from a variety of quarters: financially pressed school districts face taxpayer resistance in school bond issues and mill levy increases; teachers form unions pressuring school administrations for better working conditions and higher pay; students at the high school level express deep disatisfaction with the nature and content of the educational experience; others express serious question about the quality of education and the role of the schools in an increasingly complex society. The rhetoric of the neighborhood school confronts the reality segregated school systems. From academic quarters serious questions are raised about whether the American schools are fulfilling the promise of equality of educational opportunity. Politicians seize on the general uneasiness and exploit it for their own purposes further intensifying conflict over the role the nation's public schools should play.

The resolution resolved that: governmental financial support for all public elementary and secondary education should be provided exclusively by the federal government provides a framework to rigorously and rationally deal with the various issues confronting American public elementary and secondary education.

Note, at the outset the apparent simplification of the resolution. Superficially it appears that the affirmative resolution is directed toward a financial solution, and hence requires an examination only of the economics of public education. This view, however, does not stand up under close scruitiny. "Financial support" is inextricably linked to questions of direction (ie. deciding the objectives of policy) allocation of resources among needs, and administrative support to implement policy.

At each level questions of resource collection and resource distribution become paramount in considering either exclusive federal financial support or reliance on the current system. Hence "financial support of public education" is a two tiered process operationlized within a larger system.

The import of the above conclusion is that a consideration of the resolution necessarily involves an assessment and comparison of two systems. Initially the difference in the systems is the difference in the parameters of exclusive federal financial support implyed by the resolution and the current system. A recognition of this difference provides a point of orientation for the affirmative and negative sides of the resolution.

The first step in a consideration of the resolution consists of an examination of the current system of financial support: its scope, and limits, problems and potential.

Current federal activity as defined by legislative intent and appropriation is designed to deal with special educational needs and the support of specific national priorities, rather than general underwriting of the cost of public elementary and secondary education.

The major federal programs providing aid for public elementary and secondary education include: Public Law 815, Public Law 874, the National Defense Education Act of 1958, Civil Rights Act of 1964, Economic Opportunity Act of 1964, and the Elementary and Secondary Education Act of 1965. The bulk of federal aid for public elementary and secondary schools comes from provisions of the Elementary and Secondary Education Act of 1965. Of the approximately $2.9 billion total aid package for elementary and secondary education, some $1.6 billion comes from ESEA.[1]

Public Laws 815, providing aid for school construction, and 874, providing aid for general school operation in federally impacted areas were enacted by congress in 1950. Both acts recognized that "the federal government had a responsibility to provide money for community services in lieu of taxes because federal property is not usually taxable on a local level."[2]

Public Law 874 funds are not earmarked for specific purposes, thus placing responsibility on school administrators to allocate the funds in any manner they wish to meet the operating costs of the school districts. In 1950 $52 million was appropriated for the two bills, while $312 million was spent in 1960.[3] For 1972 the Administration projects spending $425 million through Public Law 874 and $15 million through Public Law 815.[3]

The National Defense Education Act was passed in 1958, "partly as a reaction to Soviet success in space (sputnik) and scientific endevor."[4] The uneasiness felt about the U.S. educational system resulted in the passage of the act designed to stimulate education in the areas of science, foreign language, mathematics, and other critical subjects.

NDEA is made up of ten titles of which Title III providing financial assistance for strengthing instruction in science, math and foreign language by providing grants for guidance counseling and testing directly affect public elementary and secondary education. The remaining titles of NDEA have sufficiently comprehensive to indirectly affect the operation of elementary and secondary schools.[5]

Under Title III funds have been used to construct language labs and purchase special equipment to strenthen instruction in critical subjects. Approximately $50 million will be spent in 1972 under Title III authorization.[6]

The Civil Rights Act of 1964 provides through Title VI (desegration of public education) grants to school districts to pay the cost of giving to teachers and other school personnel inservice training to deal with the problems of school desegragation as well as to pay the cost of employing specialists to advise in problems due to school desegragation. Approximately $16 million has been allocated for 1971 under Title VI of the Civil Rights Act of 1964.[7]

The Economic Opportunity Act of 1964 section 222(a) 2 provides for follow through support of the various pre-school support provissions of the bill. Head Start programs offered in the summer by OEO are continued by Head Start Follow Through. The attempt is to provide comprehensive support to other community programs. In 1969 $25 million was spent on Head Start Follow Through. The Nixon administration projects $60 million to be spent through the program in 1972.[8]

Perhaps the most important federal program designed to deal with public elementary and secondary education is the Elementary and Secondary Education Act of 1965 and its amendments. The most noteworthy provision is contained in Title I designed to provide financial assistance to local educational agencies for the education of children of low income families. Title I contains specific provisions to provide assistance to urban and rural schools serving areas with high concentrations of low income families. Explicitly the federal government has recognized the need to provide equality of educational opportunity. Other provisions of ESEA include grants for school library resources, textbooks, and other instructional materials; assistance to strengthen state and local education agencies; and funds for bi-lingual education programs.[9]

Under ESEA Title I the administration has budgeted $1.5 billion for children from low-income families; $80 million for library materials and textbooks; $143 million for guidance and testing; $10 million on drop-out prevention; $25 million on bi-lingual education; and $33 million to strengthen state and local educational agencies.[10]

Administrativily, responsibility provisions for implementing the various bills providing federal aid for education is spread throughout the executive branch. However, the bulk of funds for elementary and secondary education is administered through the United States Office of Education which is in the reporting structure of the Department of Health, Education, and Welfare.

Although the above listing of programs reflects the formal role of the federal governemnt in providing financial support for public education, it indicates little about the substansive impact of federal efforts. Thus integral to understanding the current federal role in the existing system of financial support is a consideration of the effects of federal aid on the operation of the educational system.

The specific titles of the various pieces of legislation such as ESEA maintain certain requirements that state and local governments must live up to in order to receive federal funds. Generally these requirements are expressed in terms of general guidelines, i.e. maintenance of a certain level of per pupil expenditure, income requirements of affected studnets, matching requirements etc. The specifics of drawing up a plan, and implementing and administering the plan is left to state and local governments.

The relative autonomy accorded state and local school administrators has led to compliance problems.

One scholar contends that the objectives of federal legislation are frustrated initially by the uncoordinated and piecemeal nature of the federal programs. Added to uncoordinated programs are problems in the federal delivery mechanism which rely on a top down strategy, "operating largely through administrators wielding federal-state regulations and guidelines," that, "do not have sufficient leverage to reorient classroom practice or insure that money will always reach its intended target."[11]

The record is clear that in a number of cases federal aid has missed the mark.* The NAACP legal defense fund has documented numerous instance in which Title I ESEA funds were spent for general school aid rather than for the disadvantaged.[12]

Aside from not sharing the same commitment to the legislation as their federal counterparts, part of the problem for the state and local school administrator is budgeting and accounting of funds. Having received the federal grant, the states and localities often treat it as indistinguishable from other resources thus submerging the federal intent.

To tighten up state-local use of federal funds the federal government has more closely monitered state performance, cutting of funds in some cases and even attempting to recall monies in other cases. For example, the federal government recently ordered the state of Illinois to return $3.9 million to the federal treasury for violations of ESEA Title I in 1965-66. In fact since October of 1971 the U.S. Office of Education has been trying to recall $9.1 million in federal funds allegedly misspent.[13]

---

*for example see *Schools and Inequality* (Urban Coalition, 1969) by Jame W. Guthrie, Henry Leven et. al. The authors examined in detail the school systems of Detroit and its suburbs, concluding with empirically verified evidence that neither federal or state funds were distributed equitably.

Although the federal government looms large in providing financial support for special educational needs, its total support for public elementary and secondary education is closely circumscribed. According to the National Education Association the federal governments percentage of the school dollar amounts to about 6.9 percent of the total. The remaining 93.1 percent is provided by local school districts and state governments.[14] Of the 93.1 percent, some 40 percent of school funds come from state governments and the remaining 53 percent from property tax revenues raised by the localities.[15]

State and local financial support of public education turns on two considerations. One, are local revenue collection devices fair and adequate? Two, having collected the revenues, are the states and localities able to spend or redistribute monies in a fair and adequate manner? Dealing with these two questions enables an understanding of the state-local component of the current system of financial support for public education.

At the local level primary reliance is placed on the property tax as a means of funding education. Approximately 50 percent of property tax revenues go to the schools.[16]

The property tax has come under increasing criticism because reliance on it means fewer or declining revenues in areas with declining property values, and hence less money for schools in those areas. This problem is particularly acute in overburdened municipalities in the nations urban areas. They simultaneously face declining property value and increased demands for social services. The complextion of the nation's urban schools require additional funding at a time when the ability to generate funds is falling.

One response to this problem has been the suggestion that the state governments take over responsibility for full funding of the public schools.*

Legal and social forces have contributed to and aided this suggestion finding their expression in a series of successful challenges in the courts which have maintained that the right to the "Equal Protection Clause," of the fourteenth amendment had been violated.

The first of these cases, Serrano v. Priest, and the one that all others have been modeled on was handed down by the California State Supreme Court on August 30, 1971. The California court held that reliance on the property tax to finance education was unconstitutional and directed the state of California to provide an alternative. The court did not prescribe the specific method or form the state should use. Similar

---

*See Advisory Commission on Intergovernmental Relations, *State Aid to Local Government* (April 1969)

decisions have been handed down by courts in Texas, New Jersey, and Minnesota. The Supreme Court may hear a challenge to one of these cases sometime in 1972-73.

Although it is somewhat early to consider the impact of Serranno, some initial observations can be made. First, the court's decision left a paradox due to its interpretation of equity in taxation. The same standard used to evaluate local taxation can be applied to state taxation systems. Are their revenue collection devices fair and adquate? State governments rely heavily on excise and sales taxes. On equity grounds both are regressive. However, in the face of continuing demands for public services and the apparent state reluctance to rely on the personal and corporate income tax they are necessary.

The second observation concerns the states ability to fairly and adequately distribute revenues for public education. Difficulties in state aid formulas could be overcome by specifically compensating for municipal overburden, but in light of the increasing suburban bias in many state legislatures, this seems high doubtful.

A third observation deals with the ability of state governments to hold local school districts accountable to the purpose of funding. The proximity of state governments to local needs may enhance their ability to monitor program effectiveness. However, the structure of state government and their general level of administrative ability raise some questions about their effecitveness as program administrators.

Furthermore, as previously mentioned, there may be some doubt as to the desire of state governments to meet certain national goals such as equal educational opportunity.

In fact, it is just this issue which raises questions as to the ability of any change in financial systems for schools to provide equal educational opportunity. Starting with the Coleman Report, many of the studies investigating the effectiveness of various forms of compensatory education have concluded that the nature of the problem of unequal education precludes a financial solution. Rather, as long as various socio-economic, racial and ethnic groups remain segregated, usually in the inner city, from the rest of white society, equal education will never be achieved. Consequently, the rationale is developed for changing and enlarging school district lines so as to intergrate school systems. This may not only provide for equality of educational opportunity, but also gives these school districts economies of scale for a more efficient utilization of funds; something which has occurred far more rapidly in out-state and suburban communities.

Another possible solution to this problem is busing to desegregate. Naturally, this raises the issue of President Nixon's recent moratorium on busing, and his solution, increased aid for compensatory education. This proposal may not only reopen the federal court decisions on busing which already have occurred, but also raises the question of what type of society we want: whether we want to retreat to Plessy vs. Fergusan, or reiterate our support of the 1954 Brown decision, that separate inherently means unequal.

Just such a consideration may also preclude school district reorganization and busing as viable alternatives. If school children are only involved in integragated schools for a few hours a day, but must psend the remainder of their time in the generally segregated society, can we hope for acutal improvement?

These are difficult questions which reveal the inclusiveness and depth of this topic. It has financial, social, and political dimensions that will have to be understood to debate this question effectively.

By considering these dimensions, insight into the parameters of the current system of financial support for public elementary and secondary education will be gained. Understanding these parameters enable the debater to make the comparisons necessary in either defending or denying the resolution.

[1]"Federal Share of School Expenditure at 6 Year Low," *The New York Times,* January 13, 1971, p. 1.

[2]Sidney Tiedt, *The Role of the Federal Government in Education,* (Oxford Univ. Press, New York, 1966), p. 26.

[3]*Proposed Fiscal Year 1972 Administration Budget For Programs Administered by the U.S. Office of Education,* House Committee on Education and Labor, ninety-second congress, first session, February, 1971, p. 3.

[4]*Op. Cit.,* Tiedt, p. 29.

[5]*A Compilation of Federal Education Laws,* House Committee on Education and Labor, October, 1971, p. 605.

[6]*Op. Cit.,* Proposed Fiscal Year 1972 Asministration Budget, p. 2.

[7]*Proposed Fiscal Year 1972 Administration Budget For Programs Administered by the U.S. Office of Education, p. 2.*

[8]*Ibid.,* p. 2.

[9]*A Compilation of Federal Education Laws,* Oct. 1971, pp. 23-86.

[10]*Proposed Fiscal Year 1972 Administration Budget For Programs Administered by the U.S. Office of Education,* pp. 2-3.

[11]Michael Kirst, "Delivery System for Federal Aid to Disadvantaged Children, *"Equal Educational Opportunity – 1971,* Hearings, Select Committee on Equal Educational Opportunity of the United States Senate, Ninety-Second Congress, first session, part 17, Oct. 7, 1971, p. 8617.

[12]*Title I of ESEA: Is It Helping Poor Children,* (New York: NAACP Legal Defense and Education Fund, Inc., 1969).

[13]"Illinois Told To Return School Aid," *The Minneapolis Star,* May 12, 1972, p. 16-B.

[14]*Op. Cit., The New York Times,* Jan. 12, 1971, p. 1.

[15]Harold Howe, "Anatomy of a Revolution," *Saturday Review,* November 20, 1971,p. 84.

[16]*Ibid.,* p. 85.

# CHAPTER II

## ANALYSIS OF THE DEBATE PROPOSITION

The NUEA committee on discussion and debate and the individual high school coaches are to be congratulated on their selection of the 1972-73 high school topic. Not only is our public system of education a vital issue, but the specific phrasing of the resolution provides room — lots of room — for debate. In recent years there has been mounting criticism about the phrasing of debate resolutions. One of these criticisms was that there was little difference between the affirmative and negative positions. The devil image in this criticism was always those sly, cunning framers of resolutions and that invisible majority of debate coaches who voted for them. In the past there was good basis for this criticism. The resolutions seemed to vacillate between muddy terms like "significantly increase," and "significantly change." We were caught in the "more or less" syndrome. Previous domestic resolutions called for merely "more" or "less" federal involvement, and debaters were stuck with determining the insoluable problem of degree, i.e. what was "more." Clearly this year's resolution should quiet this argument.

The 1972-73 resolution calls for *exclusive* federal federal financing of *all* public elementary and secondary schools. If there is not a clear distinction between the particular systems defended by affirmative and negative teams this year, it surely is not a problem of the resolution.

## AFFIRMATIVE ANALYSIS

This year's resolution allows a great deal of room for creativity on the part of the affirmative debater — which of course will provide both great joy and great consternation at tournaments. Except for the requisite of exclusive federal funding the entire American educational system is fair game for innovative affirmative teams. The goals of our educational system can be kept, altered, or eliminated. The present curriculum of our educational system can also be kept, altered, or eliminated. Current school districts, city, county, and state jurisdictions, can be retained, changed, or ignored. Current equations between money and education, such as student-teacher ratio or spare allocation, can be accepted, modified or rejected.

Affirmatives can create an Orwellian educational system or give complete control to the parent in keeping with the neo-populist movement. Furthermore, the affirmative may modify the common sense notions of exclusive federal financing and still be within the spirit of the resolution by defining what a "federal core curriculum" would constitute. Many services now provided by the states and localities would be excluded from the definition, leaving the states and localities free to contribute support to "fringe" programs.

It would appear that the affirmative, while accepting a large burden of proof on this year's resolution, has at least the freedom to create the educational system that makes the most sense to them.

It would appear that any affirmative case will have to speak to at least four basic questions. One, what constitutes a "good" education. Second, why should public education rely on exclusive federal financing. Third, how can federal monies best be distributed or delivered to our educational system. And fourth, in terms of effect and impact, how is the federal system of education different from the current system.

While the above questions will be dealt with in most debates, the majority of affirmative cases will tend to "focus" or "high light" certain aspects of the resolution. These cases will tend to fall within such classification as: equity cases; taxing or finance cases; planning cases; and social issue cases. Probably the easiest way to assimilate and explain these different cases is to classify them under the labels: administrative, social, and academic cases.

### Administrative Cases

The first kind of general case will be a finance case. Typically it will fixate at the level of collection of monies, and argue that federal collection is better than the current blend of federal-state-local financing. This case will discuss progressive versus regressive taxation; disparity of per-pupil expenditure between one school district and another or one state and another. Basically, this case type will tend to operate from two assumptions. First, that relatively equal sums of money should be spent on each American student, regardless of geographic location. Second, that there exists a very close relationship between per pupil expenditure and quality of education. What will distinguish one finance case from another will be the method chosen by a particular affirmative team for redistributing the money back to the actual school systems. Although this case will be common early in the year, a closer examination of what constitutes a quality education will lead to the evolvement of similar but more specific case types as debaters gain sophistication in their analysis of the topic.

Another kind of administrative analysis will be the delivery system case. This case will evolve out of a close examination of how governments distribute the taxes they collect. While the finance case focuses on collection of monies the delivery systems case focuses on the distribution of those monies.

There will likely be three kinds of distribution formulas. The first calls for redistributing money on the basis of a federal standard or criteria. This is the most prevalent form for allocating governmental monies. If an affirmative team uses a criteria formula it will probably be radically different from what is currently done.

The second basic form is redistributing tax money in the form of "block" grants to educational units. While this formula usually has some type of general criteria, it generally does not establish standards of educational content, but tends to allocate the money on a per capita basis.

The third kind of delivery system is generally some form of "voucher." For some time now, the idea of distributing education money to the student and not the school has been considered attractive. Such a delivery system maximizes individual choice and minimizes governmental control.

The ultimate acceptance or rejection of any delivery system should be judged in terms of its impact on the educational system. If efficiency is one of the elements used to assess the impact of a delivery system then still another kind of adminstrative analysis will develop. This might be labeled a jurisdictional case.

One of the ways of answering the question, "why all federal?", might be to focus upon the rather haphazard boundary lines that separate state from state, county from county, and school district from school district. Although such social issues as "busing" might be an issue in a jurisdictional case, the primary consideration of this case type will be economic efficiency. In short, the case would argue that it would make more sense to reorganize our school systems without regard for state, county, and hamlet boundary lines. Multi-city and multi-state metropolitan areas might be more efficiently organized if provincial boundaries are eliminated.

Variations of administrative cases can be developed by considering other facets of collecting taxes, delivering money to the educational system, and reorganizing school systems.

## Social Cases

If elementary and secondary education is viewed as one of the primary socializing processes in our country, and if exclusive financing is tantamount to control, then a whole new set of affirmative cases can be developed. These cases stem from the rather simple notions of who you want to go to school with and where you go to school.

The first case that centers on this emotional issue might be called the "busing" case. This case is developed from the premise that it is important to mix racial, ethnic, social, and economic groupings into each school. The justification for this blending could be made for educational, social, and national reasons. This analysis would probably be combined with some federal standards and some redistricting of school systems. Nevertheless, the rationale would not be administrative, but social.

Another way to deal with the social issue is a case that would argue directly the "federal versus state control" issue. This case would be more general than the first social case in that it would not take a stand on a particular social issue, but would simply argue who ought to control our schools — the federal government as opposed to state-local control. The basic argument of this case is that the federal government — the Congress, the Executive, and the courts — is the best governmental level to determine the social composition of our schools.

The third kind of social analysis would be one that rejected any governmental say as to who goes to school with whom and at what location. This case would argue that the parents ought to determine who their children associate with. Some sort of voucher system would undoubtedly be used. But again, the primary motive for change would not be administrative, but social.

### Academic Cases

Certainly one area of consideration within this topic is school curriculum. It would seem that at some point in the evolution of affirmative cases, debaters will begin to consider what is being taught in the school system. It may also become apparent that cirriculums differ from school system to school system. As these discoveries are made, a new set of cases will evolve.

The first type of academic case may be labeled "performance." This type of case would argue that on the basis of various achievement tests, graduation percentages, and the ratio of students who go to college, marked differences occur across populations that are traceable to specific kinds of educational systems. This case type would attempt to alter these discrepancies by the use of federal standards that would change present curriculum, methods of teaching, and means of testing.

Another type of academic case would be concerned with educational trends. By comparing what students are being taught with the skills they'll need to compete for future jobs, debaters may discover that the old army adage is true — that students are being trained for yesterday's jobs. This case would argue that national planning is needed if America's most vital resource is to be properly developed. The case would point out that many school districts seem to be unresponsive to our changing technological society. This case would merely be a fuller development of the rationale of the 1958 National Defense Education Act.

A third kind of academic case would be the "minimum guarantee" case. This case would argue that just as the federal government should guarantee minimum public assistance or minimum medical care for the aged, so should the federal government guarantee that a minimum core curriculum should be competently taught in all public elementary and secondary schools. This is your "cake and eat it, too" case. This case would standardize the academic aspects of a school curriculum, but would not stop the states and localities from adding to this "core" curriculum. As a matter of fact, one of the frustrating aspects of this year's resolution is that the resolution cannot prohibit state and local spending for education — nor can it eliminate regressive state and local taxes.

While most affirmative cases may not be presented in the forms we have suggested, certainly as a point of initial clarification it may be helpful to view this resolution from its administrative, social, and academic dimensions. Certainly, most of the above arguments will find their way into and sometimes out of affirmative cases. We will probably see an increase in the popularity of "criteria" cases. As a result we have included an article on criteria cases in Chapter IV of this book.

## NEGATIVE ANALYSIS

Probably the best advice that can be given to a negative is to know what you are defending. It's a little hard to defend the present system if you do not know what it is. Although "dynamic" and "expanding" are words that work themselves into a negative's vocabulary, it is nice if these words can be supported by argument and evidence. At first glance our current educational system appears to be an irrational patchwork of programs which are financed in a more or less helter-skelter fashion by various levels of government. However, a good debater ought to be able to provide order to this apparent confusion. A good starting point might be the defense of "diversity" as a positive good.

### Educational Goals

Regardless of the kind of educational system created by the affirmative, sooner or later (probably later) the affirmative team will have to justify its analysis in terms of some set of educational goals. They will have to demonstrate how their program moves toward these goals. One of the difficult burdens of an affirmative team will be an assessment of educational goals that can be standardized across the country.

One of the characteristics of the current system is the diversity of educational goals. In fact, outside of a few general statements, it is difficult to specify what the exact goals of our educational system are. As a result, the goals tend to be operationalized in terms of curriculum. We assume we are meeting educational goals if our economy is prospering and our society is tranquil. In the face of economic stagnation and social unrest, and sometimes because of interatnional turbulence, our

16

educational process is called into question. It may be that the entire educational system is not directly related to these economic and social issues. Education may not be either the major cause or the primary solution to economic and social problems.

In terms of the social dimension and the academic dimension of education, the recent Coleman report provides evidence to support this negative argument. At any rate, the negative should be prepared to challenge the affirmative case in terms of educational goals.

## Controlling Agent

Currently, control of our educational system is diffused throughout our society. Parents, school boards, cities, countries, states, and the federal government all share in this control. The negative may defend this "shared power" as a positive good at all levels of the anlaysis, i.e. from the financial, social, and academic perspectives. From a financial standpoint it may not be economically advisable to exclusively finance education through the federal tax structure. Although the federal tax structure is more elastic — that is revenues increase with a prosperous economy — the converse is also true, i.e., federal revenues fall when the economy declines. Therefore, while state and local taxes are inelastic, they have the advantage of not fluctuating. Thus, it may be more advantageous for financial stability for our educational system to be financed by a mixture of both tax systesm, i.e., the present system.

Also, the federal government has the primary responsibility for national defense. Recently, we experienced a trade-off between guns and butter. The negative may want to aruge that we do not want the risk of a trade-off between guns and education.

From the perspective of civil liberties, it may be undesirable to concentrate the control of our educational systems in the hands of any one governmental unit or segment of society. The current system provides many checks and balances to prevent arbitrary and exclusive control of the system. If money means control, most affirmative plans should upset this balance. The negative may well argue a successful defense of the present system by showing that current policies prevent our educational system from being dominated by any one social, religious, or political ideology.

From the academic perspective the diversity of our educational experience may once again be its saving grace. Education should not be a static notion, but an ever-evolving and changing process. If federalization breeds standardization, then the negative should be on strong ground in defending the present system. Even if we do not know what we are supposed to be teaching, we can at least keep experimenting. In the absence of the ideal curriculum, the present system is certainly preferable to the uniforming of our past and present mistakes. Many successful programs were initially conceived at the local and state level. Exclusive reliance at the federal level may remove lesser governmental levels as sources of creative programs.

## Repairs of the System

Negative repairs operate from the idea that whatever the affirmative wants to do, the negative can do better. Any sort of collection system that the affirmative advocates can be replicated by other governmental agencies or a combination of other agencies. If the affirmative wants more money the negative can raise it for them. If the affirmative wants a more progressive tax, the negative can provide it. If the affirmative prefers a "block" grant or a "voucher" system for delivering the funds, the negative has got them, too. If the affirmative wants to re-district, the negative can change jurisdictional boundaries. In short, the negative can push the affirmative into considering education from a "national" perspective with "national" guidelines. At this point, the negative can return to his blocks on controls and aruge it is not a good idea to federalize education.

## Plan Meets Objectives

Although the exclusive federal financing of elementary and secondary education may appear to be a significant structural change from the present system, in terms of effect affirmative advantages may not be significant. For example, if the affirmative isolates the harms of regressive taxes or stresses the benefits of a progressive tax system, in terms of the taxpayer's burden, the affirmative may not have made a significant change. This may be so because states retain the power to tax and there is a sizeable backlog of needed public services. In fact, in terms of the taxpayer, all the affirmative may have done is increased his tax burden.

Likewise, in terms of social and academic dimensions, the affirmative case may have no real impact as measured on the criteria of social progress or performance scores on academic tests.

Negatives should also be quick to spot a mere increase in expenditures. In other words, the affirmative spends only federal money, but perhaps its twice the amount the system now spends on education. The link between money and educational excellence may also prove to be quite tenuous. Many of the affirmative objectives may not be reachable by merely changing the collection and distribution of taxes.

Some affirmative cases may so radically change our educational system that the American parent might take it upon himself to eliminate public elementary and secondary education. If the busing issue is any indication, some affirmative plans might create federal public schools, while America's children are attending local, private schools.

Affirmative cases that stress national planning and standardization for the purposes of coordination and control may discover that the effect of their program is just the opposite. If the current federal education programs are used as models of bureaucratic efficiency, certainly an extension of that approach should be tantamount to anarchy.

## Disadvantages

Two American adages may provide the focal point for a series of disadvantages. The first is "the greater the distance between the controlling agency and the program, the greater the likelihood of failure." As evidenced by other massive federal programs, Washington, D.C. is a long ways from Muskogie, Oklahoma or Pontiac, Michigan. This, of course, has produced a dilemma for federal planners. The use of federal money without controls produces unexpected results and large federal bureaucracies are awkward and inefficient.

The other adage is "as financial commitment decreases, so does responsibility." In short, if the state and local governments are using federal money, and not their money, there will be an increase in fiscal and progessional irresponsibility. Good examples are the Army's cost-over-run spending policies and doctor's medical practices under Medi-care.

Affirmative cases which stress economies of scale should be susceptible to the natural corollary of impersonalization. Although large lecture halls, educational television, and giant supermarkets are efficient, they are also impersonal. In terms of elementary and secondary students this may become a vital issue.

Labor disputes may cause another interesting problem. Current teacher strikes are localized because they have to deal with independent school districts. If their employer is now the federal government they may well consider action at the level that the steel workers, the teamsters, and the postal workers have employed.

Of course, all the advantages that flow from a diversified educational system can be converted to disadvantages against any affirmative plan that tends to standardize the financial, social, or academic dimensions of the educational process.

Finally, while the resolution calls for exclusive federal financing, it does not call for federal statutory control of elementary and secondary education. Thus, a very destructive and debilitating clash could occur between the federal government's power of the purse, and the state's constitutional and statute powers, not to mention local and city ordinances. So, to the degree that an affirmative team's reallocation of monies alters the social and academic dimensions of education, to that degree we can expect state and local resistence. Neither the United States Constitution nor this year's debate resolution sanction the transfer of responsibility for educating American elementary and secondary students from the state to the federal level. Eventually, the arguments that are developed from this dilemma will prove decisive!

# CHAPTER III

## THEORETICAL FOUNDATIONS OF DEBATE

Debate is concerned with decision-making. In order to minimize confusion, digression, and tangential analysis, as the relative merits of any proposed social action are discussed, interscholastic debate has a clearly defined structure and process. The basic structure of interscholastic debate includes such elements as teams, speaking formats, and judges, while process includes such elements as resolution debate theory, and argument construction.

The focus of Educational Financing is primarily limited to a consideration of debate as process. In this way a practical guide to the 1972-73 high school debate topic is provided.

### DEBATE PROPOSITIONS

Interscholastic Debate involves a conflict between diametrically opposed viewpoints over "facts," "values," or "policy". The conflict centers on a particular subject that is specified by the debate proposition. One diametrically opposed viewpoint attempts to affirm the resolution, the other to deny it. Hence, the designation of affirmative and negative teams.

### Questions of Fact

A statement which asserts that something exists or is true is a question of fact. Examples: "There are 4,700 students at our school;" or "the government has access to injurious personal data about 1 of every 3 U.S. citizens." Questions of fact are always concerned with actions or events which have already occurred. The conflict on questions of fact encompasses the issue of their accuracy.

In order to debate a question of fact it is necessary to: (1) develop a standard of measurement, and (2) apply it.

If the advocate challenges the relevancy or significance of factual material, he has moved into the realm of questions of value.

### Questions of Value

A statement which attempts to make a judgement is a question of value. Examples: "Mr. Spicer is an excellent debate coach," or "separation of church and state must be maintained in all matters". In a question of value, the values are present day values.

In order to debate a question of value it is necessary to: (1) develop a standard of evaluation; and (2) apply the standard. The conflict encompasses the suitability of the standard to the situation.

Once the standard is agreed upon, the debate then becomes a question of fact centering on the application of the standard to the particular situation.

## Questions of Policy

A statement which asserts that a specific course of social action should be taken is a question of policy. A policy question encompasses both questions of fact and value as an attempt is made to establish a motive for change. Examples: "Our college should discontinue its debate team;" or "Resolved: that a voucher system should be established as the primary means of financing elementary and secondary education in the U.S."

Deliberation occurs over whether the proposed social action should be taken at some time in the future. The affirmative team favors the change and advocates the adoption of the proposition. The negative team is opposed to the change and wants the rejection of the resolution.

Debating a question of policy is not nearly so simple as debating a question of fact or value. The following sections of FINANCING EDUCATION develop concepts requisite to debating a question of policy.

FOUR CONCEPTS BASIC TO
DEBATING A POLICY RESOLUTION

### Presumption

This term is concerned with the state of the judge's or audience's mind before the debate begins. In this case, the state of mind is, at least theoretically, always in favor of the existing system — the *status quo*. Since the policy resolution calls for a change from the present system, the natural state of the judge's mind is against adoption of the resolution. Since the negative team is against adoption of the resolution presumption is said to rest with the negative.

Thus, theoretically, were a decision to be awarded prior to the start of the debate, the negative team would always win, due to the predisposed nature of the judge's mind against change from the *status quo*.

Once the debate begins, this predisposition to favor the existing system remains until some motivation is provided by the affirmative team to cause the judge to shift in opinion. This motivation is offered by the affirmative through their assumption of what is called the burden of proof.

## Burden of Proof

In any debate on a policy question, the affirmative must fulfill five basic burdens to overcome the natural presumption of the negative. These are:

1. Definition of Terms — The affirmative team must analyze the proposition and stake out or isolate the area within the topic which they are going to talk about. On the Education topic an area of concern is the inadequacy of the property tax.

2. Area of Concern — The affirmative must present a cause for action. This is accomplished by discovering an area of concern (e.g., workability of the voucher system; viability of the federal tax system; quality of education) and showing the significance of it. If the affirmative is presenting a Needs Case they must discuss the significance of a 'problem.' If they are presenting an Advantages Case they must discuss the significance of the 'benefit.'

3. Inherency — The structural weakness in the *status quo* which prevents the present system from 'solving the problem' (Needs Case) or 'accruing the advantage' (Advantages Case). For example, what is there intrinsic to the present system that creates property tax inadequacy or prevents the elastic increase of property tax revenues? The concept of inherency as it exists in the Advantages Case is called 'uniqueness.' The term refers to the fact that an affirmative davantage should be unique to the adoption of the resolution as implemented through the affirmative plan. For example, what is there intrinsic to the proposition that makes it the only policy that will enable the effective financing of elementary and secondary education? In other words, if the existing system can be shown capable of accruing the advantage, there is nothing unique about it. Thus, a nonunique advantage fails to fulfill the affirmative's burden of proving inherency.

4. New Program (Plan) — Every affirmative team must present a program for the implementation of the resolution. There are two requirements of every plan: (a) it must be under the resolution, i.e., a reasonable interpretation of the resolution; and (b) it must be a significant change from the present system, i.e., a new program. Therefore, under this year's resolution the affirmative team is required to present a program of financing that makes the system's ability to support its schools significantly different from the existing structure.

5. New Program Achieves Its Goals — For purposes of explanation, a dichotomy will be made between the Needs and Advantages Cases:

Need Case: In using a problem solution format, this obligation is usually labeled 'plan-meets-need'. The affirmative should show that the 'new program' will solve the problems which they previously indicated were an inherent part of the *status quo*. For example, would substitution for the property tax substantially increase the amount or security of the support available to U.S. school systems?

Advantages Case: In using the plan-advantages format, this obligation is usually labeled 'plan-meet (accrue or produce)-advantages.' The affirmative should show that their proposal for implementing the resolution will actually bring about the benefits enumerated. For example, that inactment of a new method of financing would substantially increase the quality of U.S. education.

Once the affirmative team has fully established all five of these burdens, they have presented what is called a prima facie reason for changing the present system's structure and adopting the resolution. At the same time, they have done all that is required of them to fulfill their "burden of proof," and to overcome the predisposition of the judge to reject change.

You have probably noticed from the above discussion that a distinction is indicated between the structure of language appropriate to discussing burdens related to the Needs and Comparative Advantage Cases. In the following section, this dichotomy is extended to a consideration of the differences in organizational development between the two types of cases in regard to the common locations of these burdens of proof.

*Location of Burdens of Proof in Debate Cases*

'Traditional Need' versus 'Comparative Advantage'

| Need Case (1st Aff Constr) | Advantages Case (1st Aff Constr) |
|---|---|
| 1. Definition of Terms | 1. Definition of Terms |
| 2. Area of Concern; developed about two or three 'needs'; each discussed in terms of:<br>a. Problem<br>b. Significance | 2. Plan<br><br>3. Area of Concern; developed about two or three 'advantages'; each discussed in terms of: |

3.  Inherency of Needs: developed
    either after each need, or in a
    separate contention

    (2nd Aff Constr)

4.  Plan (Note: frequently, the plan
    is located in the first affirmative
    constructive, especially in
    conventional 'ten-five' debate)

5.  Plan-Meet-Need

a.  Advantage
b.  Significance
c.  Uniqueness
d.  Plan-meet-advantage

    (2nd Aff Constr)

The second affirmative using the plan-advantages case has no burdens left to present. Though, further development may be necessary — particularly in the area of plan-produce-advantages

Although the above organizational dichotomy is by no means sacrosanct, it does provide a description of the more common development of the two case types. Understanding that the point at which each affirmative burden may be fulfilled is arbitrary may at this point in your reading not seem too significant. However the importance of the distinction ought to become more evident as you study case organization in relation to the Negative Burden of Rebuttal (see following section).

When the affirmative team presents all five burdens discussed in the preceding section of this book, they have presented a case which is believable and acceptable as constituting motive for adoption of the resolution. Once a *prima facie* case has been established, it can only be countered if the negative assumes its "burden of rebuttal" and offers refutation of the affirmative's case structure.

A thorough understanding of the preceding three debate concepts should provide you with a clear insight into what must be considered as you attempt to write and defend affirmative cases. The Affirmative Evidence Section in Chapter IV translates these theoretical concepts into practical issue blocks.

### Negative Burden of Rebuttal

Once the affirmative team has presented their arguments, it is necessary for the negative team to assume what is called the "burden of rebuttal" — the responsibility for offering refutation of the affirmative case analysis. In an effort to present this discussion clearly, while enabling a comparison of negative responsibilities approrpiate to debating both the Needs and Advantages Cases, the following material is presented in column form.

# Prima Facie Case

## NEEDS CASE

### 1st Negative Responsibility

Operating from a basis of presumption, present the negative rationale for things being as they are. The negative philosophy should explain the negative's approach to both the resolution and the specific affirmative case. In essence, you are laying the groundwork for all future negative refutation.

Begin direct refutation by examining the evidence presented by the first affirmative to develop the area of concern. Does the evidence actually support the problem as significant? Present evidence to minimize the affirmative's area of concern. This can be done by showing that the affirmative is mistaking the real impact of the problem, or by showing that the present system has made great progress in the particular affirmative area of concern, and currently the problem is being minimized.

In the area of inherency, the negative speaker should be sure to raise the question as to whether the affirmative's need results from a structural deficiency in the *status quo.* Moreover, he should attempt to show that the present system can and will work to solve the problem in the future. Be prepared to discuss the viability of the existing programs working to meet the problem.

In its purest sense, a negative inherency argument is one in which the negative proves that the *status quo*

## ADVANTAGES CASE

### 1st Negative Responsibility

The negative rational should be based on the premise that although the *status quo* is not perfect, it is comparatively more advantageous than the proposal of the affirmative. Develop this superiority by establishing several of the following reasons:

the affirmative advantages do not produce a significant enough improvement to warrant adoption of the debate resolution.

the advantages are not unique to the affirmative proposal in that existing programs can reap the same benefits.

the advantages cannot be produced by the specific affirmative plan.

the advantages flow from a plank in the plan which is extraneous to the resolution.

significant advantages of the *status quo* will be lost if the plan is adopted.

severe disadvantages may result that will outweigh the affirmative advantages.

Similarly, the first negative should examine the plan, initiating direct refutation in the area of:

its topicality, examining the plan to see if one plank of the plan tacitly will on its own alleviate the problem. By contrast, the minor repair attempts to establish that non-structural changes can solve the problem. Literally dozens of repairs are available on any topic. As long as the negative merely wishes to extend the usage of devices already in use somewhere in the existing structure, they are making acceptable repair of the *status quo*. If the expanded use of these devices will relieve the problem outlined by the affirmative, then the negative should feel free to 'minor repair' (of course, the negative should be prepared to show the likelihood of expanded usage). One point to remember is that all repairs suggested by the negative speaker must be compatible with one another, i.e., not mutually exclusive. It should also be remembered that negative repairs have the same obligations that are imposed on affirmative plans in that they must be 'practical,' 'workable,' and free from serious 'disadvantages'.

The negative can choose to admit the affirmative's need, and present an alternative structural change which can more easily bring about the elimination of the need. This counterplan is deemed, at least by the authors, to be a poor strategy. The difficulty in this approach stems from the necessity of the negative forsaking its presumption and attempting to prove that their counter-plan more efficiently and effectively meets the affirmative's area of concern than the affirmative's own plan.

An extension of the negative's inherency analysis, but distinguished

meets the resolution, while other planks promote the advantages.

are the critical parts of the plan truly a change from the *status quo?*

has critical evidence been presented to show that the advantages definitely flow from the plan — is there a causal link?

The first negative's next duty is to individually consider the affirmative advantages, applying the following analyses:

Is the advantage's area of concern of merit? This means more than merely asserting that the advantage is not significant. It involves proving that the affirmative's area of concern is inconsequential.

Can the advantages be gained from existing programs or through minor repairs? At this point, general evidence will not suffice. The first negative speaker must be specific, delineating the present programs and applying their critical provisions. He must cite evidence to indicate their current success and future potential.

Can the advantages be acquired from the plan? The speaker should return to his general remarks on the causal link between the plan and the advantages. He should specifically scrutinize the evidence which supports the affirmative's causal analysis. By pointing out weaknesses of the link, he will force the second affirmative to present a more complete development of this causality in order to defend the from it, is the examination of the affirmative's causal relationships. Here, the negative merely analyzes the causality between the inherent cause and the harmful effect. This is necessary because many times an affirmative will attempt to establish meet-need by minimizing the effect without eliminating the cause.

## 2nd Negative Responsibility

The second negative should examine the plan in terms of its 'propositionality' to determine if all planks of the plan are within the topic area. Examine the plan for 'duplication' of existing laws or programs — that is to see if the new program is a significant change from what we are now doing.

The most important aspect of the entire negative analysis is in the relation of whether the plan meets the need. The plan must be analyzed for any deficiency in eliminating the problem. To the extent that the proposal fails in this respect, what may be the most important affirmative burden has not been fulfilled.

Furthermore, the plan must be examined as to its workability/practicality. Here you are attempting to establish that the affirmative proposal cannot operate. A plan is normally unworkable, even though it apparently implements the resolution, when it intrinsically fails to adjust other elements of the existing society which are interrelated to the action proposed. Effective implementation of the resolution may not always be possible because of an inability to cope with the real world.

advantage. From a point of strategy, the first negative is laying the groundwork for the second negative to analyze the ability of the plan to meet the advantages. *Remember, each advantage should be individually considered in terms of the above.*

## 2nd Negative Responsibility

The second negative should continue along the lines of the first negative's plan-meet-advantages attack. If the first negative has successfully pushed the affirmative burden of proof concerning the ability of the plan to produce the advantages, then the second negative should be in a position to know exactly what support the affirmative has to support their crucial argument. At this time, the second negative should introduce evidence to enable direct refutation of the affirmative's causal link between plan and advantages.

His second duty is to present those existing benefits which will be excluded by the adoption of the resolution via the affirmative proposal. Even though it is often more difficult to determine the difference between the loss of an existing advantage and a disadvantage accruing from the adoption of the affirmative plan, this distinction is worthwhile. The authors feel that it enhances persuasion to argue that certain existing advantages will be lost as a result of changing the structure, while at the same time new disadvantages will be created.

Finally, examine the plan to isolate potential disadvantages to the adoption of the resolution — make sure that your disadvantages do not accrue from an extension of the present system; that they flow directly from the affirmative plan; and that you establish their significance with evidence.

The second negative's next duty is to present specific disadvantages to the plan. It is important to note two things: (1) quality is more important than quantity; and (2) negative disadvantages have the same burden as affirmative advantages. Namely, they must be significant, they must not accrue from an extension of the present system, and they must flow uniquely from the affirmative plan.

Once again, the authors would caution that this discussion of theory should not be regarded as prescription — the good debater is never locked irrevocably to prescription or stereotype. The above merely illustrates what each negative team member may choose to argue against the more common placements of affirmative burdens in the Needs and Advantages Cases. The major point to remember is that these same refutation responsibilities are applicable no matter where the affirmative team chooses to locate their burdens. Thus, as a negative, you only need to be able to discern the exact location of each affirmative burden and begin refutation utilizing the applicable materials indicated by the outline above.

INSTRUMENTS OF SUPPORT

Whether the debater is engaged in interscholastic or intramural competition, his purpose is to gain acceptance by presenting sound arguments in support of his viewpoint. The material which the advocate depends upon to generate acceptance of his arguments is called proof. Proof can be classified as existing in three forms: logical proof; emotional proof; and ethical proof.

### Logical Proof

Logical proof is derived from the Greek word *logus,* that is, the instrument of thinking and knowing. Consequently, logical proof is based on the process of reasoning and the use of evidence.

*Reasoning.* In academic debate, as in other areas of human understanding, the mental process of reasoning may be characterized as either inductive of deductive. The process of reasoning is inductive when the advocate picks several specific instances within a given area and moves to infer that a common element exhibited by these is also found in every other instance of that type. For example:

The debater might argue that the quality of education has been lessened by bond issue failures in Dayton, Independence and New York. He would then inductively infer that the quality of education is lessened throughout the United States.

It should be noted that the general conclusion (quality of education lessened throughout the U.S.) is valid only if the common element (bond issue failure) actually existed in each instance cited and, additionally, if the instances cited (Dayton, Independence and New York) are representative of all the other cases (all school districts in the U.S.) within the total area encompassed by the conclusion. Inductive reasoning thus moves from a consideration of the particular to a conclusion about the general.

The process of reasoning is deductive when the debater takes a statement, rule, or group of facts which relates to a general area, and applies this statement to a specific case. For example:

The debater might argue that methods of financing based on proportional rebates to districts are no better than the present local property tax system. Thus, the affirmative plan which encompasses such a financing system is deficient in accruing its advantage of more adequate financing.

Of course, the specific case (plan deficiency) is only valid if the general statement (proportional rebates to districts are inequitable) is valid, and additionally, if the specific case (the method of financing) is actually like those instances within the generalization. Deductive reasoning thus moves from a consideration of the general to conclusions about the particular.

*Evidence.* Evidence is the ingredient which serves as the basis for proof. Evidence consists of facts, lay or expert opinion, and objects or materials. Facts include anything that can be verified through experience, knowledge, or statistics. Opinion is personal testimony. Normally, lay or ordinary opinion is not accepted in academic debate as evidence. This is because the lay person has no special training or practice that would qualify him as an acceptable expert. On the other hand, expert opinion, from a person with the knowledge, training, or practice to make him an authority, is considered valid testimony and is accepted as evidence. Objects, or materials which might constitute evidence include laws and contracts.

Evidence is a necessary aid to the support and refutation of each of the burdens of proof discussed in the previous sections of this chapter. Quite obviously, with sufficient research, one can find evidence to support any position. However, evidence is not equally dependable or acceptable.

The dependability of evidence refers to the dependability of its source. Sources of evidence are often labeled primary and secondary. The general rule is the closer a reporting source is to the primary or initial source the greater the likelihood the evidence is accurate and complete — the farther away the greater the chance of distortion and omission. For this reason, government reports and congressional hearings are more dependable sources than *Reader's Digest and U.S. News and World Report.*

Similarly, the particular bias of the reporting source of evidence must be considered. The National Education Association and The American Federation of Teachers may have a particular bias intrinsic to the closeness of the education topic. On the otherhand, the intrinsic viewpoints of *Ramparts* or a particularly liberal paper may be so weighted as to taint the dependability of the evidence they report.

The acceptability of evidence is related to the utility of the evidence itself. Several criteria may prove useful for testing the utility of evidence. They are:

a. Evidence should be consistent with human knowledge and experience.

b. Evidence should relate to the overall judgement of what your audience knows, i.e., be believable.

c. Evidence should be applicable to the point you want to make and be consistent with other points in your analysis.

d. Evidence should be recent and/or pertinent to the times and the issues of the topic. Obviously, recent evidence is more likely to relate than dated evidence. However, in some instances dated evidence may be so pertinent to the issues that its use is warranted.

Evidence is used by the debater to support the conclusions which are reached through reasoning. When reasoning is coupled with evidence, the advocate has brought together the necessary elements to achieve a completed proof, i.e., support for his analysis and arguments. Evidence is differentiated from the mental process of reasoning in that evidence exists independently of the advocate-reasoning does not. Therefore, the debater *engages* in the process of reasoning, and *gets* evidence to support conclusions.

*Construction of Argument.* Reasoning and evidence are commonly combined to create five forms of argument: argument by example, literal analogy, sign, cause, and authority assertion.

1. Argument by example is one form for extending and advancing the conclusions reached through the process of reasoning. By combining these conclusions with evidence, i.e., examples of specific instances or concrete occurrences, an argument is constructed. *Sample argument:* The revenues from property tax are decreasing in many urban communities. This is true of Detroit, St. Louis, Toledo, and Atlanta.

2. Argument by literal analogy is another form for advancing the conclusions reached through the process of reasoning. Here the advocate is comparing two actual processes, or environments, or systems. The aim is to depict several respects in which the systems are alike and then infer similarity in other or all respects. *Sample argument:* The voucher system for supporting education has been successful in several pilot programs. The affirmative plan displays several similar features. Hence, the affirmative plan will also prove successful.

3. Argument by sign is also a form for advancing the conclusions reached through the process of reasoning. Here, the claim is that one event, characteristic, or condition is a predictor or indicator of a subsequent event, characteristic, or condition. Argument by sign is quite prevalent in popular discourse. "He's got long hair — he's a hippy;" "Blonds have more fun;" and "Horn-rims and a crew-cut, man, he must be a real loser" are just a few popular examples. However, on the more serious side, sign argument is used in the prediction of college and business success (grades and achievement), sickness and health (medical symptoms), and weather forecasts (clouds, pressure systems). Therefore, it should come as no surprise that sign argument will be prevalent in debating financial support for education. *Sample argument:* Bond issues are failing. The people are apathetic toward education.

4. Argument by cause is yet another form for advancing the conclusions reached through the process of reasoning. Here, the claim is that one event or condition or element is always followed by another event or condition or element, and, further, without the first event or condition or element the subsequent event or condition or element could not exist. Causal arguments will abound on this topic. *Sample example:* Archaic financing systems are the cause of inadequate school funding, or its converse, inadequate funding is due to archaic financing systems. These varied orders of presentation have been labeled "Cause-to-effect" and "effect-to-cause" respectively.

5. Argument by authority assertation is the final form for advancing the conclusions reached through the process of reasoning. Here, the advocate utilizes opinion testimony to establish an argument. Use of authority argument on this year's topic will, as always, be extensive. *Sample example:* The National Association of Manufacturers' Government Finance Department reported in 1968, "The federal tax collecting system is a marvelous instrument which operates with maximum efficiency."

*Refutation of Argument.* There are several methods for refuting each of the five forms of argument noted above. Any or all of them may prove useful depending on their applicability to the situation.

1. Argument by example. Several methods will enable you to determine the validity of this form of argument. They are as follows:

a. Question the sampling. Do the particular examples seem representative of the majority of cases? Or, are they *a typical?*

b. Are there any negative instances which contradict the conclusion? If so, cite them to establish the invalidity of the claim.

c. Are the environments the same? Do we presently have a different situation from that which existed at the time of the occurrence of the example? Similarly, is the example in the data the same as the example in the claim.

2. Argument by analogy. Refutation will stem from the following analysis:

a. Are the environments comparable. For example, is a value-added tax support system comparable to a voucher system?

b. Are the instances of similarity sufficient to warrant a claim about the whole?

c. Are there significant differences which shed considerable doubt on the analogous relationship?

3. Argument by sign. The following criteria should enable refutation:

a. Can the claim exist in the absence of the sign? For example, can people be apathetic toward education without defeating bond elections. If so, the sign argument may be weakened.

b. Can the sign exist in the absence of the claim? For example, can bond elections fail even when people are not apathetic toward education? Again, this would tend to weaken the sign argument.

c. Utilize the above points to force defense of the sign argument as a causal relation. Indict the sign argument for lacking causality.

4. Argument by cause. Three points should prove helpful.

a. Is there causality at all? Are the events only correlated, or not correlated at all?

b. Are there other factors which could offset the causal relationship. If so, suggest them.

c. Is the cause cited the first cause and/or major cause. Would multiple causality preclude the elimination of the effect, even though one cause was eliminated?

5. Argument by authority assertion. The following criteria should prove beneficial:

a. What are the authorities reasons for reaching his conclusion? Does the authority provide them, and if so, were they included in the development of the argument?

b. What do other authorities have to say regarding the issue? Is the cited authority *a typical* or prejudiced?

c. What are the authorities qualifications. Are they sufficient to make him a knowledgeable expert? Do his qualifications relate to the subject he is addressing?

## Emotional Proof

Though proof in argumentation and debate is most widely established through the use of logical-rational appeals, this is not the only means available. The advocate should practice and develop efficiency in the utilization of emotional proof. Emotional proof is derived from the Greek word *pathos*, meaning an experienced feeling. Thus, when the advocate utilizes emotional proof, he is appealing to the audience's or critic judge's feelings. Emotional proof aids the debater in producing the right attitude toward his particular viewpoint. Consider the following example: It might be argued that "more stringent controls" would create the disadvantage of "lessening the government's ability to isolate foreign agents and thus increase the problems of national defense" – the argument would appear to be solely logical. But, if on the other hand the disadvantage were worded such that "without relentless surveillance communist conspirators would defile, subvert, and finally overthrow our beloved democracy," the argument could be characterized as emotional, and capable of being experienced emotionally by your audience.

Emotional proof furnishes the advocate with a valuable means of persuasion. However, it should not be used to excess, and it should always remain well grounded in and secondary to logical argument and proof.

## Ethical Proof

Ethical proof is derived from the Greek word *ethos,* which can be defined as a listener's or critic's source of trust in and acceptance of what the speaker has to say. The concept of ethical proof is comprised of three elements: a speaker's apparent consideration for his *Rhetoric,* elaborated on how a speaker may be thought to be untrustworthy:

Either through lack of intelligence they form wrong opinions; or while they themselves form correct opinions, their rascality leads them to say what they do not think; or while intelligent and honest enough, they are not well disposed to the hearers, or audience, and so will fail . . .

The very thought of failure in academic competition should be enough to cause anyone to want to ensure that he appears intelligent, honest, and considerate of his audience.

So it is, that to gain acceptance of his position, the wise advocate utilizes more than just evidence cards. He draws on inductive and deductive reasoning in advancing his analysis, and supports his conclusions with the necessary evidence to form completed logical proofs. Furthermore, having logically established good reasons for the acceptance of his position, he calls upon the persuasive element of emotional proof to engender empathic acceptance. Finally, the perceptive debater realizes that all the good reasons in the world are not sufficient to gain acceptance if the speaker is not trusted by the audience. Therefore, he analyzes what he is doing, and attempts to ensure that what he does appears intelligent, honest, and considerate.

## RESEARCH PREPARATION

Since every debate topic calls for the implementation of some meaningful social action, the debater can always depend upon the existence of an ample supply of materials from which to draw analysis of and support for a position.

Because of the very nature of the evidence and analysis gathering process, there are several research options available to you. These options range from randomized individual reading, to structured collective evidence gathering. Both extremes have certain drawbacks — from duplicated effort to knowledge about only a limited portion of the topic. Experience indicates that for most debaters, and most debate squads, a more middle road is the best course of action.

Although it is not possible, or even necessary, for you to have knowledge about and collect every piece of evidence on this topic, this should not be confused with negating the object of research preparation. That object, of course, is to become informed enough about the surveillance to carry on knowledgeable discourse within the competitive educational debating environment. What follows is a description of a "plan for research" which, if adhered to, should enable the meeting of this goal.

The primary key to research preparation is systematization. Whether you research alone, with your colleague, or with all other squad members, your research effort must be systematized. In this manner, research duplication can be avoided, and wasted effort can be minimized.

As stated previously, there is a middle road between collective and individual research which is deemed by the authors to be best for most debate squads. Although collective in nature, this middle road incorporates certain safeguards to enable the attainment of certain benefits of individual research.

Quite obviously, five debaters can research, read, and record evidence on five times as much material as can an individual debater in the same three-hour period. Additionally, 500 evidence cards, comprising a squads research over 25 different books and articles, are better than 5 sets of 100 evidence cards each — over the same articles or books. At the same time, collective research maintains all the benefits of individual research, as long as a few simple guidelines are followed:

1. All members of the squad should be familiarized with the uses of each of the major research reference indexes.

2. All members of the squad should participate in using these indexes as a common bibliography is compiled.

3. All members of the squad should research, read, and record material within each major area of concern.

4. Each member of the squad should use the same standardized means of recording evidence in terms of, "Could I understand the relevancy of what I have recorded if I had not read the article around it?" In this manner, integrity, responsibility, and sensibility in evidence-gathering are stressed.

5. The evidence recorded from each article or book should be recorded in sequence, and kept together for a period of time to allow each squad member the opportunity of reading the evidence before it is dispersed into isolated evidence cards. In this manner, each squad member is afforded the opportunity to see all evidence in a manner which approximates the contextual relevancy of the original source.

# CHAPTER IV

## COACHES' CORNER

This chapter is designed to provide critical input from both coaches and debaters on substantive issues of debate theory and practice. For future editions of *Issues and Answers* contributions are encouraged. Send completed manuscripts to the editors, in care of Campus Press, P.O. Box 4261, Minneapolis, Minnesota.

## BEYOND THE ORTHODOX:

## THE CRITERIA CASE

### James W. Chesebro

Most of us remember the difficulties and "heated" disagreements involved in initiating the comparative advantages case. A new form of analysis at this time may produce opposite effects — sending both debaters and coaches into catatonic seizures. However, new forms of analysis should also provide healthy stimuli for debaters and coaches. Requesting that new forms of analysis be developed, Ziegelmueller has already argued that, "there is no single approach to analyzing a single proposition."[1] Thus, the major thesis of this article is that the criteria case provides a more effective and substantial approach for debating both the values and concomitant actions for a resolution.

Developed within recent years, the concept of a *criteria case* is generally applied to affirmative cases which feature value judgements as strongly as actions. In these criteria cases, the affirmative presents a set of values which are not operating within the present system yet embody the theoretical requirements of the resolution. The affirmative plan provides the mechanism to implement these values which will ultimately produce beneficial actions for society. The essential focus of the criteria case, then, is upon value judgments as well as actions.

There is theoretical justification for considering an analysis which equally features and emphasizes values as well as actions. Traditionally, argumentation theorists have recognized the significance of value judgments in a proposition of policy in both the problem-solution and comparative advantages approaches. Glen Mills underscores the importance of values in the problem-solution approach. He argues that, "a proposition of policy involves facts and values plus considerations of practicality, expediency, and action."[2] Indeed, the concepts of "harm," "evil," or "ill" clearly imply a concern for value judgments. Discussing the problem-solution approach, Donald Torrence aptly summarizes the point: "The stock need issue in a proposition of policy is clearly a question of value."[3] Likewise, the comparative advantages approach features value judgments used implicitly to measure and govern the actions stemming from a proposition of policy. Brock argues that the advantages affirmative:

> must demonstrate that some principles, which are included in the present system and are expanded in the affirmative plan, are related to or are the causes of gaining an accepted goal of the present system.[4]

The terms "principles" and "goal" appear to be equated to value judgments in this analysis. But more overtly, Ziegelmueller has observed that the advantages affirmative may equate its goal or principles to the terms *criteria, subgoal or value.*[5]

Using this perspective, the purpose of this article is to outline one form of analysis which would feature and require that both the value and action steps of a resolution be more equally, systematically, and substantively debated. In developing this thesis, a four-fold analysis is employed: (1) a rationale for the criteria case is offered; (2) philosophical assumptions relevant to a criteria case are outlined; (3) *prima facie* requirements for a criteria case are provided; and (4) implications of the case are discussed.

## Rationale

Although several reasons might be offered for an analysis which features values and actions equally, three reasons are examined here. First, from a theoretical perspective, the criteria case provides an opportunity to determine the *prima facie* requirements for a proposition of value. In most argumentation textbooks, specific procedures and methods for justifying new values have been ignored. Most argumentation theorists recommend criteria and an application of the criteria in an analysis of values. However, theorists have not provided the specific procedure or steps to be used in justifying the new criteria or applying the criteria to a particular situation. Note how one writer suggests analyzing values:

> The preliminary, analytical questions which would be useful in the search for potential issues in a proposition of value might be phrased this way: Upon what criteria should the evaluation be based? How well does the matter to be evaluated measure up to these criteria?[6]

These questions are then followed by an extended example in which the questions are rephrased in terms of a football game. The analysis closes by noting that our values emerge through our cultural heritage because of the social good they serve. Such an analysis can be of little help to a debater or a debate coach. The essential set of *prima facie* steps necessary to select, justify and apply the criteria are missing. Note the conclusion reached by Brock: "Some writers recommend criteria and application in the analysis of questions of fact and value, but they do not provide specific steps for this analysis."[7] Because the criteria case emphasizes values and actions equally, theorists are forced to indicate the specific steps necessary to establish new values.

Second, from a practical perspective, the criteria case seems justified because it would force debaters to analyze substantively, attach, and defend values as a structural part of an affirmative analysis. Debaters are currently either ignoring or unsure of the methods for sustaining attacks and defenses of the issues of value in debate resolutions. The criticism becomes clear in the exchange between two superior teams, Wichita State University and the University of Houston. Mr. Thompson, the first affirmative for Wichita, initially established the goals or values toward which the affirmative intended to make comparative improvement with their proposal. He argued:

> In June 1966 the Advisory Council on Public Welfare reported to the Secretary of Health, Education and Welfare that the elimination of poverty and the achievement for all its people of social justice, basic security, and opportunities for self-realization are the announced goals of the Great Society. To further those goals, Bob and I resolved that the federal government should guarantee an annual cash income to all citizens.

Mr. Ware, the first negative from Houston, asked:

> First of all, Dave and I would like to ask the gentlemen just exactly what the goal of their proposal is? If they want to increase the living standards, the living conditions, of the poor? We want a definite statement there.

Mr. Shields, the second affirmative, responds:

> I think Lee substantiated the particular goals that we are talking about in his first speech when he noted that the elimination of poverty and the achievement of all its people of social justice, basic security, and opportunities for self-realization are the announced goals of the Great Society. We're trying to achieve those objectives. We suggest that the affirmative proposal can do just that.

The initial negative question becomes the basis for the second negative plan attack by Mr. Seikel. He argues:

> Let's go back to the affirmative goals, they don't provide a justification for their specific deduction scale. They talk about $1500 per adult and $1500 for the first three children, etc. I want to know what the justification is for those specific amounts. More important, they never tried to correlate it to a poverty line which would be required for an adequate standard of living.

The first affirmative responds:

> The specific justification for our deduction scale – we provide the social capital that the gentlemen from Houston are so fond of talking about. Loretta Daniels says that the parent who is given a chance to substantially supplement the family income, is given the decision of family responsibility.

The issue is concluded by the second negative – the argument is dropped by the second affirmative:

> We have already observed that providing increased cash above the poverty line, i.e., social capital doesn't get at those social and psychological consequences. I don't think that was really responsive.[8]

The value issue in this example is clearly initiated by the first negative and then used by the second negative. A legitimate set of issues could have been exposed: *How was the value selected by the affirmative? Why was it selected? What justification exists for it being the nation's highest priority for dealing with poverty?*[9] *What are the operational characteristics of the value? How does one measure or know when one has achieved the value?* However the value issues become "clouded" and slip to a concern for mechanics of the plan and later to the credibility of an affirmative advantage. The nature of the claim, the warrant and the data essential to establish the goal or value are submerged. Both attack and defense shift away from the value issue. The structure and requirements of the comparative advantages case and the problem solution case do not require that the affirmative and negative react to values in an overt method.[10]

Third, consideration of the criteria case seems justified because it would more realistically feature the significance of the value itself as part of policy formulation. In both the United States domestic and foreign policy, the isolation of a value is viewed as the key to the actions implicit in the policy itself. The value judgment itself sometimes receives more attention than the accompanying action steps. In addition, the criteria case is especially well adapted to a consideration of policy priorities. Note the very real consideration given to the question of priority by the Council of Economic Advisers: "Choices will have to be made – not to solve one problem at the expense of another, but rather to allocate resources in such a way as to permit balanced progress on many fronts."[11] While we may not agree with the Council, the statement is a very credible example of the concern expressed for policy priorities. The criteria analysis, which would feature values and their significant structural limitations and relationships, would be more responsive to such a legitimate question of values and value priorities.

## Philosophical Assumptions

Two philosophical assumptions relevant to the criteria case are considered here. First, we shall assume that value judgments and changes are culturally derived. Richard McKeon states the argument:

> . . .the expression of values has its basis in the circumstances and forms of expression of a times; and the potentialities of circumstances are expressed in ideal realizations . . . The common values which unite men of different times and places are given different expressions appropriate to, and determined by, their respective periods and cultures.[12]

Value judgments, then, would be viewed as emerging from cultural circumstances, needs and adjustments in the criteria case.

The second relevant assumption is that value judgments are accepted by a culture if the value is an accurate appraisal of past reality and also an insightful perspective for evaluating future events, as far as they may be predicted. Seldom does a culture adopt a value which cannot and will not enhance the development of the culture. Gibson Winters argues that the basic issue is the priority of *sociality* in which value judgments are adopted only if, "man grasps" his past, present situation, and looks to the future determining if social identity and potentiality are enhanced.[13] As a philosophical assumption, then, the adoption of a value in the criteria case presupposes that the social order of the past, present and future support or are enhanced by the value proposed.

## Prima Facie Requirements

Employing the philosophical assumptions in a more pragmatic fashion, four procedural issues emerge which would be addressed in the criteria case. These four issues are:

1. *What are the operational features of the value?*
2. *PRESENT: What new social relationships, changes or structures are required to adopt the value today?*
3. *PAST: How would these new social relationships have affected or enhanced society in the past? or Would these new social relationships be more consistent with our understanding of past events?*
4. *FUTURE: Will the new social relationships enhance the society? Will these new social relationships be more consistent with predicted future events?*

Although several orgizational patterns might be employed, the four issues may be featured in the case structure below.

I.  *Statement of the criterion to be adopted.*
  A.  *Define the operational features of the value:*
    1.  *Establish the necessary or essential individual characteristics of the value.*
    2.  *Demonstrate that the operational features of the value require the adoption of the debate resolution.*
  B.  *Identify the scope of institutions, and actions of society affected today:*
    1.  *Describe or establish the nature of the environmental adjustment.* (Not a statement of improvement per se.)
    2.  *Demonstrate that the environment can reasonably undergo such an adjustment – other significant values or actions are not lost.* (This issue may be initiated by the second negative as plan attack.)
  C.  *Demonstrate that the new relationships established by the value is or would have set into motion a better set of controls or actions for the past and present, or that the new value is consistent with an accurate description of changing events.*
  D.  *Demonstrate that the new relationships established by the value would set into motion a better set of controls or actions for the future.*

With this structure as a framework for analysis, several descriptive observations are warranted. Turning to the "statement of the criterion to be adopted," the statement itself should be a carefully worded statement in which the value advocated appears as a desirable motive for change. Strategically, the terms featuring the value should allow the judge to associate the advocated value with other acceptable, significant and constructive values of the present system. The statement of criterion, then, ought to create a favorable attitude toward the action proposed yet also state the degree of improvement foreseen.

After stating the criterion to be adopted, the affirmative must "define the operational features of the proposed value." Most theorists distinguish universal characteristics (descriptive terms that apply to more than one concept) and essential or necessary characteristics (terms that apply to only one concept). The obligation of the criteria affirmative is to demonstrate that their definition accurately identifies the essential features of the proposed value yet also requires the adoption of the philosophical intent of the resolution. At a 1969 summer high school workshop, one team developed the analysis in this fashion:

> Bill and I believe that Congress should prohibit unilateral military interventions. By United States unilateral military interventions, we mean deployment of U.S. troops in the intra-state affairs of another country. Also note that covert aggression is an insurgency from within a nation supported by an external power. Overt aggression is an armed attack by one country upon another. With these definitions in mind, Bill and I believe that we can enhance the U.S. position among other nation-states. However, to accomplish this, we do believe that more carefully selected objectives must first be initiated. We believe a controlling standard for

assessing and determining foreign policy ought to be that: *Nationalistic independence enhances our foreign policy* [repeated]. Consider four points of initial analysis.

First, let me define nationalistic independence. Nationalistic independence will be defined as that condition which exists when the citizens of a state have a sense of committment to preserve the sovereignty of their nation. This would ultimately enhance our foreign policy because it would keep the country independent of any foreign control or domination.

Second, let me argue that nationalistic independence is a major and significant goal of our foreign policy. This was indicated by Robert S. McNamara . . . However, we believe that unilateral military interventions undermine the growth of nationalistic independence. That brings us to point three.

Three, in principle, unilateral military interventions and nationalistic independence are diametrically opposed. By definition, when a major power intervenes in another country, controls its economy, society and/or politics, nationalistic independence is lost. Samuel Huntington points this out. . . . Therefore, we can see that in principle, unilateral military interventions and nationalistic independence are diametrically opposed. What's more, they are opposed in practice. That brings us to our fourth point.

Four, unilateral military interventions and nationalistic independence are opposed in practice. For substantiation of this, we can turn to two typical areas of the world: Lation America and Southeast Asia. . . .

Because of these four conditions, we propose the following plan to do away with United States unilateral military interventions. . . .[14]

The second obligation of the criteria affirmative is to "identify the scope of institutions, policies and actions of society affected today." Because change is an "ordeal" for most people, the policies, institutions and new value priorities created must be reasonable and carefully described. The changes resulting from the proposed value ought to be viewed, then, as a statement of control and as a basis for integrating potential negative attack.

The third obligation of the criteria affirmative is to "demonstrate that the new relationships established by the value are or would have set into motion a better set of controls or actions for the past and present." The guidelines for developing this line of analysis might closely correspond to a problem-solution analysis but greatly reduced in scope. It is not, however, always possible to indicate that a value adopted today would remove problems of the past. As a result, the affirmative may select a second option and demonstrate that the "new value is consistent with an accurate description of changing events." For example, a debater may wish to argue that military interventions by the executive are a waste of resources *today* because Communism is polycentric. However, he may find it difficult to argue that military interventions were a waste of resources when Communism was monocentric in the 1950's. As a result, criteria affirmatives may find two options beneficial. They may (1) argue that new values could have avoided past and present problems, or (2) that the new value is more responsive to changing events.

The fourth and final obligation of the criteria affirmative is to "demonstrate that the new relationships established by the value would set into motion a better set of controls or actions for the future." This line of analysis forces the affirmative to predict the impact of the proposed value. Such a future prediction may require a comparison between current values and actions and the new values and action proposed by the plan. Depending upon the resolution the affirmative would most likely maximize or minimize trends currently occurring in society.

## Implications

The criteria analysis would affect theoretical considerations in the field of argumentation as well as the affirmative, negative and the critic-judge. Turning first to the implications of the criteria analysis in the field of argumentation, it seems essential to consider the uniqueness of the criteria case. Generally, the criteria case would focus upon definition of values or goals while the comparative advantage case would focus more directly upon predicting future effects on the environment. However, criteria analysis may also allow the affirmative to identify and justify *new* values as a response to environmental changes. The comparative advantages case, on the other hand, rests upon the assumption that the affirmative is making progress toward established values within the present system. However, these arguments avoid the central concern of this writer. *The central issue is how to ensure that debaters effectively and substantively debate questions of value and value priorities.* From this perspective, the criteria case is best viewed as a restructure of the comparative advantages case or the problem-solution case or as a structure that would allow debaters to debate effectively and overtly the values accompanying the actions implicit in a resolution. Torrence captures the point:

> The value position of the affirmative is usually implicit and seldom stated. Negatives with similar values unconsciously accept the implications. However, "real-life" ethical disputes frequently center upon this very value dimension. Teachers would be remiss if they did not point out this

two-dimensional nature of need issues and if they did not teach their students how to treat questions of value. The demand for value statements to be directly supported by evidence is naive. If we do not know how to support value statements, we had better learn how it is done.[15]

The criteria case also has implications for affirmative teams. Because the analysis overtly advocates exposing values, most affirmatives would have to be prepared for negative attacks that deny the value and value priorities of any affirmative case. The defense of the value may require that the affirmative argue that other values are: (1) consistent with the value proposed or (2) that other values should be rejected, or (3) the new value should have priority, or (4) that the net gains of the new value exceed the loss of other values.

For the negative the criteria case may require that a more overt statement of interrelated values be defended and that the desirability of a more limited set of values proposed by the affirmative be denied. While the defense of present values and value priorities may require an assessment of values in terms of the past, present and future, the negative might strategically consider arguments for values which are not based on circumstances — a major assumption of the criteria analysis. In context, Ziegelmueller has aptly concluded that negative teams might challenge affirmative criteria by (1) rejecting the goals or subcriteria of the affirmative; (2) rejecting the primacy of the value or; (3) redefine the value.[16]

For the critic-judge the criteria case represents the introduction of new value issues, but essentially his basis for a decision remains the same. He may expect the affirmative to argue that their proposed values are significant and consistent with past, present and future events. The negative is likely to defend a larger or broader set of interrelated values. Ultimately, however, the basis for the decision remains the same. The critic-judge determines which team did the better job of debating both the value system and the resulting actions. As before, the rational decision would be whether the beneficial effects of the proposed change are greater than harmful effects.

### Summary and Conclusion

While it seems appropriate to consider an anaylsis which equally features values and actions as structural features of a debate case, argumentation theorists have failed to describe the steps necessary to establish a proposition of value. As a result debaters have not substantively attacked and defended value judgments in either the problem-solution and comparative advantages cases or in the newly emerging cirteria case. The *prima facie* requirements and implications of the criteria case described here seem well suited to debating value arguments while also preserving confrontations on the actions implied by a resolution.

*James W. Chesebro (M.S., Illinois State University, 1967) is a Ph.D. Candidate and Teaching Associate in the Department of Speech, Communication, and Theatre Arts, University of Minnesota, Minneapolis, Minnesota.* This article is reprinted from the Winter 1971 *Journal of the American Forensic Association* with the permission of the author and publisher.

[1]George Ziegelmueller, "The Logical Responsibilities of the Comparative Advantages Case," paper read at the Central States Speech Association convention, April 19, 1969.

[2]Glen E. Mills, *Reason in Controversy* (Boston, 1964), p. 55.

[3]Donald L. Torrence, "Need Issue Includes Value Judgment," *Speaker and Gavel*, IV (November 1966), 6.

[4]Bernard L. Brock, "The Comparative Advantages Case," *Speech Teacher*, XVI (March 1967), 120.

[5]Ziegelmueller.

[6]Mills, pp. 101-102.

[7]Bernard L. Brock, "Selecting National Debate Questions," *Journal of the American Forensic Association,* V (Spring 1968), 46.

[8]Tape recording of the quarterfinal elimination round, March 8, 1969, Heart of America Debate Tournament, Tournament Director Donn Parson, Department of Speech, University of Kansas, Lawrence, Kansas.

[9]The priority of the affirmative plan was also a major issue in this debate. While the negative argued that the affirmative plan required a Vietnam withdrawal which had not been justified, the affirmative argued that the domestic significance of the advantages justified such a military change. Again, the affirmative priority of proposed values were neither justified nor substantively denied.

[10]It is also observed that presently constructed criteria cases fail to assume the full burden of proof such an analysis implies. Criteria affirmative generally present a list of new criteria to be used as guidelines for effective policy decisions, but the criteria employ value terms with an extremely high level of abstraction and neither the judge nor negative team is confident of the operational meaning of the criteria. The priority of these new criteria is seldom discussed nor are reasons offered by the affirmative for why the criteria should be employed or why alternatives are not better suited to effective policy. Negatives generally counter the affirmative criteria by offering a new set of equally abstract criteria. See the University of Redlands affirmative used in the preliminary and elimination rounds at the National Debate Tournament in 1969, National Debate Tournament, DeKalb, Illinois, April 14-17, 1969, Tournament Director Roger Hufford, Department of Speech, Clarion State College, Clarion, Pennsylvania. Also see the M.I.T. affirmative at the same tournament, the Oklahoma State affirmative at the Wichita State Debate Tournament, November 22, 1968, and the Emory University affirmative at the Emporia Debate Tournament, October 24-26, 1968.

[11]Council of Economic Advisers, *Economic Report of the President,* January 1967, p. 138.

[12]Richard McKeon, "Communication, Truth, and Society," *Ethics,* LXVII (January 1967), 96.

[13]Gibson Winters, *Elements for a Social Ethic, Scientific and Ethical Perspectives on Social Process* (New York, 1966), pp. 219-220.

[14]William Cahoy and Terry Powers, Final round of competition, June 27, 1969, High School Debate and Forensic Workshop, Department of Speech, Concordia College, Moorhead, Minnesota. Workshop Director was James W. Chesebro.

[15]Torrence, 7.

[16]Ziegelmueller.

# PROOF IN DEBATE

## Gerald H. Sanders

Since I believe that proof is a most important element of academic debate, and since various scholars take different views toward proof, the basic purpose of this paper is to determine a consensus definition of proof as it applies to academic debate.

It is surprising that so many argumentation and debate texts avoid giving a general definition of proof. In most cases, the discussion of proof is found in the various evidence sections. In fact, the newest edition of one of the most widely used debate texts only alludes to such a definition when the author, Austin J. Freeley, posits that, "The combination of premises with reasoning is the proof of the conslusion."[1] This allusion,contained in a discussion on the nature of reasoning is not inclusive enough because it does not consider proof in terms of acceptance by a particular audience. In Freeley's chapter on evidence, various types of proof are treated as forms of evidence. This approach to argumentation and debate would seem to be consonant with the older texts which devote many pages to evidence but few pages to proof.

The two concepts which seem to create a dichotomy in arriving at a general, contemporary definition of proof are (1) the concept that proof must be generated by formal logic and (2) the concept that proof is determined by its acceptance by a particular audience.

Perhaps Glen E. Mills has discovered the basic weakness in any definition of proof that fails to realize the complex implications of such a definition. Mills argues that one should not limit a definition to the projected beliefs of some unspecified listeners or to some critical standards. In his book, *Reason in Controversy,* he discusses proof in terms of five conceptions. These conceptions are: need-fulfillment; consonance with a climate of opinion; empirical verifiability; logical demonstration; and, a combination of substantive and structural factors to satisfy disinterested, intelligently critical listeners or readers.[2] It is felt that a brief explanation of each of these conceptions would add substance to the basic thrust of this paper.

The conception of need-fulfillment refers to the psychological need some people have to believe an idea. This need causes them to accept, uncritically, any expression of this idea. For instance, when a prominent newspaper published excerpts from the now famous *Pentagon Papers,* a Department of Defense study of this country's involvement in Vietnam, there were those who believed so deeply that former President Johnson was a deceiver in office that they accepted, uncritically, the newspaper's editorial opinion that Johnson had deceived the American people. No thought was given, by these people, to the possibility that these printed excerpts from the study might have been quoted out of context. The newspaper's allegations gave certain people psychological reinforcement and "proof" that they were right about Johnson all the time.

The conception of consonance with a climate of opinion relates closely to the conception of need-fulfillment. However, a person's conscious assessment of what constitutes proof is inherent to the conception of consonance with a climate of opinion. For instance, there was a time when the general belief was that the world was flat. To the people who held this belief, the accomplishments of Columbus and Marco Polo did not disprove this precept. The definition of proof constructed by Ehninger and Brockriede seems to relate to Mills' conception of consonance with a climate of opinion. These authors posit that, "Proof is the process of securing belief in one statement by relating it to another statement already believed."[3] The implication here for students of argumentation and debate is that a particular audience must receive proof that is consonant with their beliefs before it is accepted.

The conception of empirical verifiability refers to proof by reference to experience. Mills says that verification can be either direct or indirect. "The shape of the earth has become directly verifiable in the Space Age, but the exact language of Patrick Henry's 'Liberty or Death' speech remains indirectly verifiable."[4]

The conception of logical demonstration relates to the use of formal, structured logic. An example here would be any argument structured in the form of the classic syllogism.

The conception of a combination of substantive and structural factors to satisfy disinterested, intelligently critical listeners or readers is a combination of the third and fourth conceptions with the resulting persuasion being rather restricted. The combination of reliable knowledge and valid inference would seem to be a strong form of proof. However, Mills points out the weakness of this conception when he says, "This means that persons who are normally critical would be excluded from this category in cases of biasing personal interest in the outcome."[5] For example, a member of organized labor may be normally critical in his thinking. However, he would still disbelieve any logical presentation of an argument for a Right to Work Law.

The realization that any definition of proof has many complex implications does not mean that we should abandon our pursuit of such a definition as it relates to argumentation and debate. Therefore, let me offer a rationale for pursuing this matter. Whether it is in academic debate where two teams are seeking a favorable decision from a third-party judge or a platform situation where an advocate is seeking to influence the belief and/or action of an audience, the speaker or speakers are trying to secure a favorable response to their argumentation. Audience acceptance, then, should be a basic criterion on which we base our definition of proof. This is not new thinking. Baker and Huntington made the following statement in a book published in 1925:

Just as certain subjects suggest at once the idea that the nature of the subject is a most important means of persuasive adaptation, so certain audiences compel attention to the equally important adaptation suggested by the nature of the audience.[6]

William Trufant Foster underlined this belief in the second edition of his book published in 1936 by saying:

Therefore the final test of any piece of evidence — a definition, a citation of authority, an inference — is never its sufficiency for the one who employs it, but its sufficiency for those to whom it is addressed[7].

Foster further states that, "Argumentation is concerned not only with rational grounds for belief, but with all other grounds for belief."[8]

Therefore, the definition I propose for proof as it applies to argumentation and debate combines the concepts of reasoning and audience acceptance. The definition is this: Proof is argument correctly reasoned to support a conclusion and designed to secure the acceptance of a particular audience. An argument can be perfectly structured with consistent evidence and reasoning but unless it is acceptable to the particular audience to whom it is addressed, it is not proof in a contemporary sense. Both the evidence and the reasoning must be selected and structured in a manner acceptable to the particular audience involved. The audience can be a single debate judge or a hundred people.

[1] Austin J. Freeley, *Argumentation and Debate,* Third Edition, (Belmont, California: Wadsworth Publishing Co., Inc., 1971), p. 112.

[2] Glen E. Mills, *Reason in Controversy* (Boston: Allyn and Bacon, Inc., 1968), p. 39.

[3] Douglas Ehninger and Wayne Brockeriede, *Decision by Debate* (New York: Dodd, Mead & Company, 1967), p. 99.

[4] Mills, *Reason in Controversy,* p. 41.

[5] *Ibid.*, pp. 43.

[6] George Peirce Baker and Henry Barrett Huntington, *The Principles of Argumentation* (Boston: Ginn and Company, 1925), p. 277.

[7] William Trufant Foster, *Argumentation and Debating* (Boston: Houghton Mifflin Company, 1936), p. 113.

[8] *Ibid.*

# CHAPTER V

## AFFIRMATIVE & NEGATIVE BLOCKS

### Affirmative Blocks

I.  EXCLUSIVE FEDERAL RESOURCE COLLECTION INSURES AN ADEQUATE LEVEL OF FUNDS FOR PUBLIC ELEMENTARY AND SECONDARY EDUCATION.

A.  Public elementary and secondary education requires increased funding.

1.  Public educational costs have continued to climb.

"Report of the Commissioners Ad Hoc Group on School Finance," *Equal Educational Opportunity – 1971,* Hearings, Select Committee on Equal Educational Opportunity of the United States Senate, 92nd Congress, 1st Session, Part 16D-3, "Inequality in School Finance," September-October, 1971, p. 8354b.

"Over the past 10 years, expenditures for public elementary and secondary education have been increasing at a rate 43% higher than the increase registered for the economy as a whole. The 10 year annual growth rate of 9.7% for total school expenditures compares with a rate of 6.8% for GNP (both in current). The 1963-68 growth rate in educational expenditures per capita is 2.75 times the rate of increase in personal income per capita. The 1969-70 increase of 10.4% in school expenditures was 4.3 percentage points higher than the 6.1% gain in GNP."

– IBID., p. 8354b.

"The total cost of public elementary and secondary education has more than doubled in the past ten years, increasing from $15.6 billion in 1959-60 to $39.5 billion in 1969-70. Total elementary and secondary educational expenditures including current expense, capital outlay, and interest, rose from $35.8 billion in 1968-69 to 39.5 billion dollars in 1969-70 for an increase of 10.4%. During this same period the total current expenditure, the largest and most significant component of which is teachers' salaries, increased from $29.0 billion to $32.3 billion for an increase of 11.2%. An increase in enrollment in public elementary and secondary schools from 36.3 million to 45.7 million from 1960 to 1969 was a cause for part of the total increase in expenditures for public elementary and secondary education. A projected figure for 1975 indicates a further increase to 46.4 million."

– "School Crisis Builds Despite Stable Rolls," *The New York Times,* November 29, 1971, p. 50.

"A spokesman for New York City schools, where the operating budget tripled to more than $1.5 billion from the beginning to the end of the last decade, expects costs to continue to rise even though it is projected that the city's birth rate and school population will fall."

— *IBID.*, p. 50.

"Despite the stabilization in enrollments, it is believed that expenses and inflation will force outlays for education to rise by at least 25% in the nineteen-seventies."

— *Equal Educational Opportunity* — *1971*, Hearings, Select Committee on Equal Educational Opportunity of the United States Senate, 92nd Congress, 1st Session, Part 16D-3, "Inequality in School Finance," September-October, 1971, p. 8588.

"School costs . . . have continued to climb nearly 10% a year — far more rapidly than property values in most communities. Property taxes are the largest single source of school revenue. During the last school year, local taxpayers shelled out 52% of the $42 billion spent on public elementary and high schools."

2. Enrollment Demands are Concentrated in High Cost Urban Areas.

— "School Crises Builds Despite Stable Rolls," *The New York Times,* November 29, 1971, p. 50.

"Among the reasons that school expenses are expected to go up in cities — perhaps even while enrollments drop — is that as the more affluent families continue to flee to the suburbs a larger portion of the urban school population is being made up of disadvantaged youngsters. . . . It costs more to provide such children with an education that is equivalent to that given to those who are not disadvantaged, said Dr. Kenneth Buck, secretary of the Council of Big City School Boards of the National School Boards Association."

— "Report of the Commissioners Ad Hoc Group on School Finance," *Equal Educational Opportunity* — *1971*, Hearings, Select Committee on Equal Educational Opportunity of the United States Senate, 92nd Congress, 1st Session, Part 16D-3, "Inequality in School Finance," September-October, 1971, p. 8362.

"Because of the escessive costs of non-educational governmental services in central cities, the educational share lags behind that of non-educational expenses. This simply means that the competition for the property tax dollar for the urban school district is greater than for its non urban neighbor."

— James W. Guthrie (Assistant Professor, U. of California, Berkeley), *Equal Educational Opportunity,* Hearings, Select Committee on Equal Educational Opportunity of the United States Senate, 91st Congress, 2nd Session, Part 7, "Inequality of Economic Resources," September 30; October 1, and October 6, 1970, p. 3404.

"Suffice it to mention, for example, the cost of obtaining school sites in central cities where land is sold not by acre or lot, but by the square foot. Price differences such as this mean that the city district's school dollar is not only harder to come by, but that it also tends to purchase less."

— Council for Economic Development, *Education for the Urban Disadvantaged,* March, 1971, p. 68.

"The cities must provide massive educational services in order to place their disadvantaged children on a par with more advantaged suburban peers. All the special programs for the disadvantaged . . . tend to be more costly than programs ordinarily required for other children. This is certainly true of compensatory and remedial programs. More youths in the inner city are enrolled in technical-vocational courses than in the suburbs, and the cost of such programs is estimated to be generally 35% higher than the cost of academic high school courses."

3.  The demise of non-public school enrollments further exacerbates cost pressures on public education.

   a.  Political, legal and economic developments have led to a decline in non-public school enrollment.

      — "School Aid Upset in Pennsylvania", *The New York Times,* April 7, 1972, p. 14.

      "A Pennsylvania law compensating parents for tuition paid for pupils in nonpublic schools was declared unconstitutional here today by a three judge Federal court.

      The court said the law had made it possible to use funds raised by taxes to subsidize religious education. All but 250 of Pennsylvania's 1,500 nonpublic schools are Roman Catholic."

      — *Ibid.,* p. 14.

      "Last January 11 a panel of three Federal judges sitting in New York City voided a 1971 state law that allocated $33 million a year to church-related schools for secular education services for pupils in nonpublic schools.

51

The judges said that the law which authorized state payments for teacher salaries and other costs for secular subjects in parochial schools, was substantially similar to three other state laws that the United States Supreme Court declared unconstitutional in June, 1971."

– "Cahill Retreats on Parochial Aid," *The New York Times,* April 20, 1972, p. 15.
"Governor William T. Cahill announced here today that he was abandoning his legislative proposals for providing $12 million in state tuition grants to the parents of private and parochial school students in New Jersey. The Governor, a Republican, said that he had acted reluctantly in response to two recent Federal court decisions that held that such tuition grants for parochial school students violated provisions in the Constitution for the separation of church and state."

– *Ibid.,* p. 15.
"The Governor's initial parochial school aid program amounted to $9.5 million last year and created a stormy controversy in the legislature. Opponents contended that it was unconstitutional at best and at worst siphoned off funds that should be going to the hard pressed public schools."

– "School Aid Upset in Pennsylvania," *The New York Times,* April 7, 1972, p. 14.
"Immediately after the Federal judges here had rendered their decision, bills were filed in Albany proposing alternatives. Among them was one by Senator John D. Caemmerer, a Nassau County Republican, under which the state would pay aid directly to the parent of a child in a parochial school.

It would provide payments adjusted to the income of the parent, with a maximum of $250 for a high school child whose parents had a taxable income under $4,000. However, the approach in that bill has not found favor in the past with Governor Rockefeller on the ground that such a direct aid plan would increase in cost each year, as tuitions rose, with a consequent pressure on lawmakers being exerted by Catholic parents."

– "Report of the Commissioners Ad Hoc Group on School Finance," *Equal Educational Opportunity – 1971,* Hearings, Select Committee on Equal Educational Opportunity of the United States Senate, 92nd Congress, 1st Session, Part 16D-3, "Inequality in School Finance," September-October, 1971, p. 8358.

"Enrollment in private elementary and secondary schools has decreased from 5.9 million in 1960 to 5.7 million in 1969, with a projected enrollment of 5.4 million in 1975. Private school enrollments comprised 10.9% of the total in elementary and secondary schools in 1950 and rose to a high of 14.9% in 1959. Since that time there has been a rather consistent decrease so that preliminary figures indicated that in 1969 only 11.1% of the total enrollment in the elementary and secondary schools were enrolled in private schools. Every indication is that the total enrollment in the private schools and their percentage of total enrollment is elementary and secondary schools will decrease."

— "Nixon vows to aid Catholic Schools, but asks Caution," *The New York Times,* April 7, 1972, pp. 1; 14. ". . .the President said," if the nonpublic schools were ever permitted to go under in the major cities of America, many public schools might very well go with them because they simply couldn't undertake the burden.

—"Cahill Retreat on Parochial Aid," *The New York Times,* April 20, 1972, p. 15.
". . .supporters contended that the parochial school system was vital in a state in which 20% of the entire student population attended private or parochial schools. They argue that many schools (in New Jersey) would be threatened with imminent closing if they did not receive new aid, thus forcing thousands of their students into public schools . . .already overcrowded."

—"School Crises Builds Despite Stable Rolls," *The New York Times,* November 29, 1971, p. 50.
"Part of the enrollment slack in public schools will probably be offset by the entry of pupils from non-public schools. Enrollment in Roman Catholic elementary and secondary schools fell from 5,198,326 in 1967 to just under 4 million in the current school year."

4.  The Structure of the Educational Labor Force exerts continual upward cost pressures.

    a.  The Labor intensive nature of the Educational work force precludes productivity advances.

        —"Report of ʾe Commissioners Ad Hoc Group on School Finance," *Equal Educational Opportunity—1971,* Hearings, Select Committee on Equal Educational Opportunity of the United States Senate,

92nd Congress, 1st Session, Part 16D-3, "Inequality in School Finance," September-October, 1971, p. 8356.

"Another reason for its rising costs is that education has proven intractably to be a labor intensive activity. The possibilities of substituting (possibly) cheap capital goods for dear labor in educational processes has turned out to be extremely limited, so far, Moreover, labor in education has become dear, first as enrollment increases outran increases in numbers of newly trained teachers and second as teachers have succeeded in organizing themselves into powerful bargaining units. . . .In the private sector firms are able to make labor more productive as the price rises on substitute capital for labor; in the public sector labor costs rise with little or no increase in productivity. Moreover, there is no incentive (profit or otherwise) in schools for this substitution."

-IBID., p. 8358.

"The per pupil costs in the Catholic schools, which comprise the largest segment of private education, are increasing more rapidly than those in public education. This is caused by a number of factors and is in spite of the fact that the total cost per pupil in Catholic elementary and secondary schools is typically less than half that of the local public school. The major reason for the increased costs of Catholic education is the replacement by lay teachers, who are prone to request the going market salary of the public school teacher, for the diminishing number of religious teachers whose stipend for teaching service has historically been very small."

-IBID., p. 8358.

"The National Catholic Education Association has reported a 10% enrollment decline since 1967. They also report a decline in the number of schools of 7% during the same period. At the same time there was a decrease of religious teachers in their schools of 12% and increase of 16.6% in their operating costs to a total cost of $1.4 billion in 1969-70. As the enrollment and percent of total enrollment decreases in the private schools, the public schools will have to absorb the additional students and their educational program costs."

b.  The Decline in Non-public School enrollment increases cost pressures on the Public Schools.

-"Nixon Heartens Church Schools," *St. Louis Post-Dispatch*, April 9, 1972, p. 3-c.

"President Nixon said the nonpublic schools enroll 5,200,000 children, and Catholic schools account for 83% of that total. If these schools vanished, American taxpayers would have to pay an additional 3 billion dollars a year for public school operating costs. New classrooms would cost up to 10 billion dollars. President Nixon, using figures from the final report early last month of the President's Commission on School Finance, said that if the nonpublic schools closed, 70% of the burden would fall on the seven states of California, Illinois, Michigan, New Jersey, New York, Ohio and Pennsylvania."

–IBID., p. 3-c.
"The Philadelphia archdiocese, including the city and four suburban counties, has 278 parish elementary schools and 32 diocesan high schools. The number of children being served is 230,000 – about 12% of them black – and the annual budget is $80,000,000. Philadelphia's public school system has 290,000 children – about 56% of them black – and an annual operating budget of $365,000,000."

c. The educational labor force has increased its economic demands exerting further upward cost pressure.

– "Financial problems plague schools across the Nation," *The New York Times,* March 15, 1971, p. 31.
"The increasing cost of public education is attributable partly to inflation and partly to an increased demand for services. But mostly it can be laid to the rapidly rising salaries of teachers.

Over the decade, in many cities, teachers' salaries caught up with those in other professions. In Philidelphia, for instance, the average annual teacher's salary went from $5,000 a decade ago to $11,300 today.

While in most cities the collective bargaining agent for teachers, wherever there were unions or associations, became increasingly powerful over the decade, school systems without collective bargaining kept pace with the salary increases. In St. Louis, for example, the average salary rose from $7,557 five years ago to 10,500 dollars this year."

–"Report of the Commissioners Ad Hoc Group on School Finance," *Equal Educational Opportunity–1971,* Hearings, Select Committee on Equal Educational Opportunity of the United States Senate, 92nd Congress, 1st Session, Part 16D-3, "Inequality in School Finance," September-October, 1971, p. 8357.
"Salaries of teachers have in the past, and will continue in the

future, to be the most important component in size and percent of annual increase, of the educational budget. It is difficult to ascertain the specific implications of teachers' salaries upon budgeting for education in the future. Suffice it to say however, that the increased organization, militancy and unionism of the teachers could easily lead us to predict that there will be increases in teachers' salaries in the future and that they will in all likelihood still comprise as large a portion of the total educational budget as they do at the present time."

—James W. Guthrie (Assistant Professor, U. of California, Berkely), *Equal Educational Opportunity,* Hearings, Select Committee on Equal Educational Opportunity of the United States Senate, 91st Congress, 2nd Session, Part 7, "Inequality of Economic Resources," Sept. 30; Oct. 1, and 6, 1970, p. 3405.

"It is no mere coincidence that powerful teachers organizations have tended to rise initially in the big cities. The flow of middle class parents from the cities has frequently created an educational power vacuum. The remaining parents often did not pay close attention to the operation of the schools. Consequently as teacher militancy gained momentum, there was little by way of a countervailing political force to hold it in check. Now many of our big city systems appear to drift almost helplessly, buffeted by the self-seeking demands of powerful teacher organizations and unable to require greater productivity for the outlays of additional remuneration."

B.  Current Needs for Funds Exceed the Ability of Existing Collection Arrangements.

1.  Public education is financed to a significant degree by property taxes.

—"Inequities seen in School Funding," *The New York Times,* November 3, 1971, p. 53.
"98% of the school revenues raised by local districts comes from the property tax."

—"Revision is urged in School Finance," *The New York Times,* September 19, 1971, p. 45.
"During the last school year, local property taxes accounted for 55.5% of the money spent on public elementary and secondary schools."

—"Report of the Commissioners Ad Hoc Group on School Finance," *Equal Educational Opportunity—1971,* Hearings, Select Committee on Equal Educational Opportunity of the United States Senate, 92nd

Congress, 1st Session, Part 16D-3, "Inequality in School Finance," September-October, 1971, p. 8361.

"Quite clearly the local school district has had to assume the major responsibility for raising taxes to finance the increasing costs of public elementary and secondary education. The property tax continues to be the primary and in most instances, nearly sole revenue source over which the local school district has any discretionary authority. The share of distribution of property taxes for local school districts has risen from 32.9% in 1942 to 50.2% in 1969. In the process of securing a major portion of revenue raised by the local property tax, the school district has displaced all other local governments as the chief claimant for local property tax dollar."

2.  Property taxes are an inadequate means of raising revenues for public education.

    a.  Property taxes are inelastic.

        −IBID., p. 8361.

        "Part of the cost-revenue squeeze presented earlier is caused by the relative in elasticity of the property tax. Property tax expansion depends in large part on the state of the housing market and the lag in assesments. Recently (1968-70) the housing market has been slow in terms of new construction and remodeling. Consequently, Richard Netzer estimates tax elasticities for 1968-70 as follows:

        | | |
        |---|---|
        | Property tax (or less in housing recessions | 1.0 |
        | Sales Tax | .9-1.0 |
        | Federal income tax | 1.6 |
        | State income tax (National average) | 1.7 |
        | N.Y. State income tax | 2.0 |

        −*Equal Educational Opportunity − 1971*, Hearings, Select Senate Committee on Equal Educational Opportunity of the United States Senate, 92nd Congress, 1st Session, Part 16D-3, "Inequlity in School Finance," September-October 1971, p. 8579.

        "The inelasticity of the present system of taxing real estate for school support is a major shortcoming. The property tax base, unlike a tax on income, expands very slowly and does not follow the business or income cycle."

— James Maxwell (Professor of Economics, Clark U.) *Financing State and Local Governments,* Brookings Institute, 1965, p. 76.
"State-local revenues depend heavily on sales and property taxes. The yields of these taxes are much less responsive to economic growth than income tax yields, which are dominant in the federal revenue system."

—John Due (Professor of Economics, U. of Illinois) *Government Finance: Economics of the Public Sector* 1968, p. 376.
"The Revenue elasticity of (a) . . .tax, that is, the response of the tax yield to changes in national income vary from 0.8 to 1 for the property tax in recent years, . . .compared with the income tax which varies from 1.1 to 1.4."

—Joseph Pechman, *Federal Tax Policy,* Brookings Institution, 1966, p. 203.
"At constant tax rates, state and local taxes are barely rising in proportion to the gross national product, while the rate of growth of expenditures is at least 20% faster than the GNP growth rate."

b.   The shifting property tax base precludes adequate funding.

—"Report of the Commissioners Ad Hoc Group on School Finance," *Equal Educational Opportunity–1971,* Hearings, Select Committee on Equal Educational Opportunity of the United States Senate, 92nd Congress, 1st Session, Part 16D-3, "Inequality in School Finance," September-October, 1971, p. 8367.
"Many of the roots of the crisis in financing large city educational programs may be found in the redistribution of population and various economic developments that have taken place during recent years. These changes have left the poor, undereducated, aged and non-white in the central cities and have taken heavy manufacturing, many retail establishments and other kinds of business activity to the suburbs along with middle and upper income families. The obvious result has been the inability of the tax base of the cities and income level of its residents to meet the high cost educational and other needs of the population in the city. The population and economic shifts from central cities to the suburbs have combined to depress the income base of the central cities relative to their suburbs and have caused a much slower growth in the urban property tax base. For the nation as a whole suburban property growth rate in recent years has been more than two and one-half times that of the the central cities. The growth on a per capita basis is the key point."

*–Report of the National Advisory Commission on Civil Disorders,*
1968, p. 283.
"Meanwhile the decay of the central city continues – its revenue
base eroded by the retreat of industry and white middle-class
families to the suburbs, its budget and tax rate inflicted by rising
costs and increasing number of dependent citizens and its public
plants, schools, hospitals, and correctional institutions deteriorated
by age and long deferred maintenance."

*–IBID.,* p. 329.
"Local government have had to bear a particularly heavy financial
burden...All United States cities are highly dependent upon
property taxes that are relatively unresponsibe to changes in income.
Consequently, growing municipalities have been hard pressed for
adequate revenues to meet rising demands for services generated by
population increase. On the other hand stable or declining cities have
not only been faced with steady cost increases but also with a
slow-growing or even declining tax base. As a result of the
population shifts of the post war period, concentrating the more
affluent parts of the urban population is residential suburbs while
leaving the less affluent in the central cities, the increasing burdens
of municipal taxes frequently falls upon that part of the urban
population least able to pay for them."

–"Report of the Commissioners Ad Hoc Group on School Finance,"
*Equal Educational Opportunity–1971,* Hearings, Select Committee
on Equal Educational Opportunity of the United States Senate,
92nd Congress, 1st Session, Part 16D-3, "Inequality in School
Finance," September-October, 1971, p. 8372.
"Continuing with Detroit as an example, we must observe its tax
base is actually decreasing. Assessed valuation dropped from
$20,000 per pupil in 1960 to $16,500 in 1968. This is a
consequence of a variety of factors: industry moving to sites outside
the city, urban renewal projects which replace tax paying buildings
with public structures, and freeway construction which destroys
taxable property."

*–Report of the Advisory Commission on Intergovernmental Rela-
tions,* April, 1969, p. 35.
"Despite the wide scope for improved administration of the
property tax the fact remains that this tax has a relatively sluggish
response to economic growth – certainly when compared with the
personal income tax. As a result of this sluggish response and
growing expenditure demands, local governments are continuously

pressured into the search for additional tax dollars. Further increases in effective property tax rates, however would only add to the already notable demand for property tax relief – evidenced by programs in Minnesota and Wisconsin to provide relief to the elderly and by formal and informal tax concessions granted by localities themselves."

c.  Jurisdictional competition constrains the availability of revenues from state tax sources.

–Walter Heller, (Professor of Economics, U. of Minn.), *New Dimensions of Political Economy,* 1967, p. 126.
". . .interstate competition and fears of losing industry and wealth, not only inhibit state-local taxing efforts, but push them in regressive directions. In speaking of this destructive and self defeating tax competition, Ecker-Racz notes that although 'the influence of tax considerations on the location decisions of business is grossly overstated. . .its impact on state and local taxation is not.' I doubt that he overstates the case when he says: 'Fear of losing business to another jurisdiction haunts the mind and stills the pen of the state and local law maker, and special pleaders have developed the skill of exploiting this fear to a high art.' "

–Harvey E. Brazer, "Federal State and Local Responsibility for Financing Education," *National Educational Finance Project,* v. 2 1970, p. 250.
"The smaller the taxing jurisdiction within the federal structure of government in the United States, the more susceptible it is to the loss of industry, commerce, and wealthy individuals in response to local differentials in tax levels. Local school districts are likely to be constrained in their taxing effort by this consideration."

3.  Bonds are an ineffective means of financing public education.

a.  Bonds are primarily used for limited purposes and nonrecurrent capital improvements such as facilities.

–John Due (Professor of economics, U. of Illinois) *Government Finance: Economics of the Public Sector* 1968, p. 305.
"State and local government borrowing is primarily employed to finance nonrecurrent capital improvements lasting over a period of years. Of necessity long-term bonds are issued to avoid the problems of constant refunding, which could prove disastrous because these governments have no power to create money or control over

monetary policy. The typical policy is to issue bonds for roughly the period of the expected life of the investment or somewhat shorter. . ."

b.  The use of revenue bonds (i.e., bonds which are not taxpayer obligations, rather they are met from revenues from the investment) require state and localities to pay higher interest rates.

   *–IBID.,* p. 306.
   ". . .revenue bonds require payment of a higher rate of interest, often about one percentage point."

c.  The use of general obligation bonds invites a taxpayer revolt, frustrating financial support for public education.

   –"Harold Howe II (former U.S. commissioner of education) "Anatomy of a Revolution," *Saturday Review,* November 20, 1971, p. 87.
   "Many of the school districts in the deepest fiscal difficulties are those of the new middle income and blue collar suburbs that must raise almost all their school funds from taxes on housing. These districts often have more children per residence and little or no industrial and commercial tax base. The result is a lower assessed valuation per child than in wealthier suburbs and some urban areas. While incomes are well above the poverty level in blue collar suburbs, property taxes are high, school costs are mounting, school expenditures are frequently inadequate, and taxpayer revolts against spending more on schools are increasing."

   –"Financial Problems Plague Schools Across the Nation" *The New York Times* March 15, 1971, p. 15.
   "Bond issues for schools are also being rejected at a record pace. According to the investment Bankers Association, only 48% of the school bond issues were approved at the polls last year, compare to 77% in 1965."

   –"Taxpayer Revolt Raises A Dilemma," *The New York Times,* January 10, 1972, p. 4.
   "Taxpayers across the country are openly resisting paying more to support municipal and educational programs even though many of the programs stem from requests made by these taxpayers themselves-as homeowners, businessmen and parents of school children.
   In three New Jersey school districts voters rejected referendums last month for building progtams. In Portland, Oregan, two

consecutive school levies were rejected, forcing an early close for the school year. In Chicago, a $22.8 million cut in educational expenditures has been ordered."

4. States and localities lack adequate remedies to improve revenue collection.

—William Henderson, Helen Cameron (Ohio State University) *The Public Economy*, 1969, p. 209.
"...the property tax is the only important tax available to the localities. The only feasible alternative — the income tax and the retail sales tax — cannot be successfully administered by any but the large municipalities."

— *Report of the National Advisory Commission on Civil Disorders*, 1968, p. 283.
"The problem has many dimensions — financial, political and institutional. Almost all cities — and particularly the central cities of the largest metropolitan regions — are simply unable to meet the growing need for public services and facilities with tradition sources of municipal revenue. Many cities are structured politically so that great numbers of citizens — particularly minority groups — have little or no representation in the process of government. Finally, many cities lack both the will and the capacity to use effectively the resources that are available to them."

— Joseph Pechman, *Federal Tax Policy* Brookings Institute, 1966, p. 232.
"Even if they make a substantial effort of their own, the state and local governments will be unable to meet their growing needs without substantial federal assistance. Part of this assistance will come from conditional grants, which will help finance activities in which the federal government has a strong interest. But the states and local governments will also need financial help for other state-local programs. As the nation faces up to the enormous tasks of improving education, providing welfare and health facilities, and reconstructing the blighted areas of its cities, a new program of supplementary federal grants for general purposes becomes an increasingly urgent."

C. Exclusive Federal Collection of Revenues would better insure sufficient Funds to meet the Needs of Public Education.

1. The Federal government relys to a significant degree on the personal and corporate income tax.

— Joseph A. Pechman, *Federal Tax Policy,* Brookings Institution, 1966, p. 1.
"The most distinctive feature of the U.S. tax system is that it places great weight on the individual and corporation income taxes. They account for over 45% of total revenues of all levels of government. At the Federal level they account for over 60%."

2.  Reliance on the federal income tax would provide adequate revenues for public education.

    a.  The Federal income tax is more elastic.

        — Walter Heller (Professor of Economics, University of Minnesota) *New Dimensions of Political Economy,* 1967, p. 65.
        ". . . in a growth context, the great revenue-raising power of our federal tax system produces a built-in average increase of $7 to $8 billion a year in      ; federal revenues . . ."

        — *IBID.,* p. 127.
        "In contrast to Federal Reliance on growth — responsive taxes . . . states and localities depend largely on taxes that respond sluggishly. They draw nearly four-fifths of their total tax revenues from sources — property taxes (45%) and sales and growth receipts taxes (33%) — whose yields at stable tax rates barely keep pace with the growth of the economy, rising a trifle less than 10% for every 10% rise in the GNP."

        — *Revenue Sharing and It's Alternatives,* Subcommittee on Fiscal Policy of the Joint Economic Committee, July, 1967, p. 233.
        "An expenditure elasticity of 1.7 and revenue elasticity of 0.9 or 1.0 leave a financing gap that is the perennial fiscal problem of the states. At the Federal level the situation is entirely different. The GNP elasticity of Federal expenditures appears to be considerably less than that of State expenditures. The elasticity of Federal receipts by all indications appears to be in the same neighborhood as the elasticity of expenditures — 1.1 or 1.2."

    b.  Federal income taxes are not restrained by jurisdictional competition.

        — "James Q. Wilson (Professor of Political Science, Harvard) *The Metropolitan Enigma,* 1967, p. 327.
        ". . . states are in a competitive position, one with the other and must be wary of increasing taxes or redistributing income in a way

that will enable neighboring states to attract away industry. Only the Federal Government is not in this competitive position."

II. EXCLUSIVE FEDERAL RESOURCE COLLECTION INSURES A MORE EQUITABLE MEANS OF PROVIDING FOR PUBLIC ELEMENTARY AND SECONDARY EDUCATION.

A. Present methods of school finance rely to a significant degree on regressive taxes.

– Walter Heller (Professor of Economics, University of Minnesota) *New Dimensions of Political Economy,* 1967, p. 136.
"Out of the $28 billion increase in state and local tax revenues between 1955 and 1965, 44% came from increased property taxes, 34% from increased sales and gross receipts taxes, and only 14% from individual income and corporate income taxes. Coupled with sharp reductions in Federal income tax rates during the same period and increases in social security payroll taxes, the increases in state-local taxes are moving us in a regressive direction. In sketching the national fiscal blueprint for the future, do we really want to design an overall Federal state-local tax system in which – to put it in extremes – we dismantle the progressive and comparatively equitable Federal income while leaning ever more heavily on the regressive and comparatively inequitable state-local property, sales and excise taxes."

– John F. Due, (Professor Economics, University of Illinois) "Alternative Tax Sources for Education," *National Educational Finance Project,* v. 2, 1970, p. 297.
"Income is typically regarded as the best measure of taxable capacity, and total net wealth as a secondary acceptable measure. But the property tax is not closely correlated with either. The portion of the property tax on homes distributes the tax burden on the basis of the gross value of one particular kind of property. Since there is a wide dispersion of ratios of such property to income or net wealth, there is substantial departure from accepted criteria of equity. Specifically, the tax places a disproportionate burden on persons owning their homes but having little current income, and on those having relatively high portions of their total wealth in taxable form. The effect is a severe burden on older persons owning their homes, on families with incomes temporarily reduced, and on persons who prefer to spend relatively high percentages of their incomes on housing."

B.  Present methods of finance for public education rely on inequitable tax assessment.

– *IBID.*, p. 297.
"Because of uneven assessment, lack of uniformity of valuation results in different tax burdens on persons owning equivalent amouns of property. Innumerable studies have shown the dispersion in assessments, even when efforts are made by assessors to do a careful job. The difficulty is in part inherent in the tax. Other levies are imposed on flows – on income or sales. Since the property tax is imposed on the value as of a particular time, constructive valuation is required. This is not difficult with some property but it is very troublesome with others."

– "Report of the Commissioners Ad Hoc Group on School Finance," *Equal Educational Opportunity – 1971,* Hearings, Select Committee on Equal Educational Opportunity of the United States Senate, 92nd Congress, 1st Session, Part 16D-3, "Inequality in School Finance," September-October, 1971, p. 8367.
"Of great concern to many educators and most tax authorities is the percent of market value of the property tax. Here again we see a wide divergence among states from 7.9% on a market value $19,000 house in Newark, New Jersey to 0.56 percent for the same value home in New Orleans, Louisiana. More important, because substantial funds come to local school districts from sources other than the property tax, is the total tax burden as a percentage of income in the states. The variance here is from 16.6% of the $3,500 adjusted gross income for a family of four in Maine in 1968 to 3.1% of the $50,000 adjusted gross income in Washington. It is such statistics that vividly indicate the nearly universal regressivity of state and local taxes and the concomitant necessity for securing funds from the progressive federal income tax to assume a larger portion of state and local financial burdens."

– Terry Sanford (former Governor of North Carolina) *Storm Over the States,* 1967, p. 26.
"If the states have failed to provide adequate state revenues to aid local government, they have also been slow to straighten out the inequitable and jumbled administration of local property taxes. Tax valuations are frequently unrealistic and unfair. Most states require theoretically, that assessments be uniform, but in too many states eqalization of valuations is not required or not enforced. Assessments vary from community to community. In New Jersey (before it was corrected) the assessed valuations were found to vary from 16 to 56% of true value, in Pennsylvania from 20 to 78%, and in Washington from 13 to 38%. In states which receive a portion of the property tax collections, there is positive encouragement to competitive under assessment as means of minimizing local contributions. Half the states

distribute grants in aid on formulas based on local wealth as evidenced by the assessed values. This sytem penalizes correct assessment and rewards under assessment."

C. Present methods of finance for public education rely on an inequitable tax burden.

    1. The tax burden is inequitable on an interstate basis.

        — "Report of the Commissioners Ad Hoc Group on School Finance," *Equal Educational Opportunity — 1971,* Hearings, Select Committee on Equal Educational Opportunity of the United States Senate, 92nd Congress, 1st Session, Part 16D-3, "Inequality in School Finance," September-October, 1971, p. 8362.

        "Recognizing the relative importance of the property tax in supporting education in most states, it is also interesting to note the great variance in per capita property taxes among the states. The range in 1968 was from $33.90 per capita in Alabama to $226.18 in California. It is also of interest to note that the per capita property as a percent ratio to the total per capita state local taxes varies from a low of 16.6% in Alabama to a high of 61.0% in New Hampshire. And finally, it is perhaps most meaningful to see the ratio of property taxes to personal income in the states where the range is from 1.58% of personal income in Alabama being consumed by the property to 6.92% of personal being consumed by property taxes in Wyoming."

    2. The tax burden is inequitable on an intrastate basis.

        — Arthur Wise (Associate Dean, Graduate School of Education, University of Chicago) "The California Doctrine," *Saturday Review* September 20, 1971, p. 78.

        "The problem to which the case was addressed can be simply stated by an example. The Baldwin Park school district expended only $577.49 to educate each of its pupils in 1968-69, while the Beverly Hills school district, in the same county, expended $1,231.72 per pupil. The principal source of this inequity was the difference in local assessed property valuation per child: In Baldwin Park the figure was $3,706 per child, while in Beverly Hills it was $50,885 — a ratio of 1 to 13. Furthermore, Baldwin Park Citizens paid a school tax of $5.48 per $100 of assessed valuation, while Beverly Hills residents paid only $2.38 per $100 — a ratio of more than 2 to 1."

        — Arthur E. Wise (University of Chicago) *Rich Schools Poor Schools* 1968, p. 127.

        "The local share of the education bill is primarily from taxation of the real property located in the district. Hence, the power of some districts to include estates or large industrial holdings within their boundaries but to exclude high-density residential areas allows those districts to provide expensive education at extremely low tax rates. The other result, of course, is that the poorer districts (in terms of local real property base) must levy taxes at high rates in order to finance even a minimum program. The gerrymandering of the real property base excludes a substantial portion of local wealth from the support of schools."

D. State and local governments are inherently unable to provide for an equitable means of funding public elementary and secondary education.

   1. State revenue needs preclude the development of non-regressive/progressive taxes.

      a. The Federal government preempts the income tax base.

         — Walter Heller, (Professor of Economics, University of Minnesota) *New Dimensions of Political Economy,* 1967, pp. 127-8.
         "Limited state reliance on income taxes reminds us of a fourth barrier, namely, heavy Federal reliance on selected tax sources. References to the Federal preemption of the income tax are not uncommon. . . . it seems clear that the high Federal income tax does inhibit the states and localities in the use of this progressive tax source, for how else would one explain the virtual halt in state income tax enactments in the 1940's and 50's."

         — Joseph F. Zimmerman (Professor of Political Science, University of New York) *State and Local Government,* 1968, p. 236.
         "More than 35 states levy a corporation income tax; twenty states allow the deduction of federal taxes in computing net corporate income. Rates vary from 1% on incomes under $1000 in Arizona and on incomes under $3000 in Arkansas to 8.4% on the income of national and state banks in Minnesota. State corporation income taxes yielded in excess of $1 billion in 1960, approximately 6% of total state tax revenue. Local corporation income taxes yield less than $10 million annually. The income tax generally is considered to be the tax which most accurately reflects ability to pay, but heavy federal income taxes limit severely the amount of taxes which the state and the city governments can derive from taxing income."

b. States are forced to rely heavily upon the property tax.

— William Henderson, Helen Cameron (Ohio State University) *The Public Economy,* 1969, p. 182.

"Five considerations favor continued large-scale use of property taxation by local governments: 1) capitalization has absorbed much of the tax's past inequalities; 2) the tax, as it applied to real estate, has been well administered by most local governments; 3) it is a major revenue producer for local governments, and equal or worse drawbacks attach to possible substitutes; 4) it absorbs some of the increments in real estate values resulting from general economic growth; 5) although some localities may have pushed effective rates of their levies to constitutional or economic maximums, most can still expand revenues from this source because of new building and rising prices."

c. The reduced revenue base spawns additional regressive taxes.

— Otto Eckstein,
*Public Finance,* 1967, p. 61.

"The variety of tax bases is a result of government's perennial need for more money. When expenditures increased more than the revenue produced by the tax system, governments look for new sources, which usually means new tax bases. It has also been argued that excessive reliance on any one base produces adverse economic effects. Therefore, a tax system may do less economic damage if it raises moderate amounts from several bases rather than large amounts from one or two."

— *Advisory Commission on Intergovernmental Relations,* April, 1969, p. 8.

"Because localities rely so heavily on the property tax, demands have been generated for additional state aid financed, as it generally is, from nonproperty tax sources — the general sales, personal and corporate income as well as other nonproperty taxes."

— Ira Sharkansky (Professor of Political Science, University of Wisconsin) *The Politics of Taxing and Spending,* 1969, p. 14.

"The state income tax appears to be progressive in the lower income ranges ($0-3,999); regressive from $4,000 to $7,999; proportionate from $8,000 to $9,999; and then progressive to the uppermost range . . . When the burden of the $2,000-$3,999 income class is compared with that of the $15,000 class, the state income tax shows a slightly regressive character. The varying burdens of this tax reflect the great variety of rates, exemptions, and income brackets that are used by different states. And the low rate of the highest income group reflects the fact that most state taxes reach their highest rates at a relatively lower income figure. In 1962 only eight states had a progressive rate structure above $15,000, and only three states (Delaware, Maryland and New Mexico) had a progressive rate structure above $30,000. In all other states, the very rich paid the same proportion of their income . . . as did the citizens in the middle income ranges."

2. The complexities of property tax administration precludes equitable assessment.

   a. Property tax administration is highly fragmented.

      — Council for Economic Development, *A Fiscal Program For a Balanced Federalism,* June, 1967, p. 31.
"The present local administration of the property tax is generally inadequate. The legal responsibility for assessing property for tax purposes rests with officials in about 18,000 primary assessment jurisdictions, many of which are too small to permit the employment of professional assessors. Assessors are often elected officials who lack technical competance. Because of inadequate staffing, reassessments are made infrequently and inaccurately."

      — *Advisory Commission on Intergovernmental Relations,* April, 1969, p. 35.
"While important gains in the quality of property tax assessments have been made, it is also clear that much more action along the lines outlined in this Commission's 1963 report is urgently needed. Nationwide, the average overall level of realty assessment has risen only from about 29% in 1961 to about 31% in 1966. In a majority of states, at least half of the local assessing areas covered in the latest Census still had a dispersion index for one family house assessment of over 20%. The Census data also showed once more a marked divergence in most parts of the country in the assessment for various kinds of realty, usually including a much lower assessment ratio for vacant lots than for improved urban property. Thus, there is still a long way to go to make the property tax — now yielding some $31 billion a year — a more equitable revenue instrument for governmental financing."

b.  State and local units face legal-political limitations.

— Council for Economic Development, *A Fiscal Program for a Balanced Federalism,* June, 1967, pp. 32-33.
"States frequently place constitutional restrictions upon local taxing and borrowing powers in the form of maximums allowable in relation to assessed value of taxable property. These limitations have impaired the ability of local officials to tax, borrow and plan effectively. Constitutional property tax and debt restrictions are incompatible with governments responsive to the needs of our rapidly growing and shifting populations."

— *Advisory Commission on Intergovernmental Relations,* April, 1969, p. 36.
"In the competitive struggle to capture the property tax dollar school officials have had to overcome indirect as well as direct limitations to the property tax base. One such indirect limitation relates to the effect of the assessment base on school revenues. Obviously, assessments at a fraction of full value necessitate higher rates to produce a given yield. While most state constitutions provide for assessments at full value, this requirement is honored more in the breach than in the observance. Even in those states where an attempt has been made to legislate current assessment practice into basic state law, assessments typically fall below the legal standard simply due to the passage of time. Assessors cannot revalue all property every year. Thus even though an assessor may appraise property at 25% of actual value, rising values mean that within a short time the assessed value will constitute less than 25% of full value."

c.  State and local governments lack uniform and equitable tax assessment standards.

— Council For Economic Development, *A Fiscal Program for a Balanced Federalism,* June, 1967, p. 32.
"It is common practice to assess improvements more heavily than land in relation to market value, business property more heavily than residential property, and new property more heavily than old property. Thus the property tax is not proportional to the value of the property as intended by law. These practices reduce incentives to rehabilitate property and to use urban land efficiently."

— *IBID.,* pp. 31-32.
"Improper assessment procedures have led to gross inequities. (1) Within individual assessment jurisdictions individual properties of a

like category are often assessed at widely varying ratios of market value. (2) Within individual jurisdictions inequities exist in the treatment of different categories of property. Inequities resulting from poor assessment administration are frequently compounded by attempts to assess property on the basis of current earnings rather than market value. (3) Although the distribution of state grant in aid and shared taxes is frequently based upon the assessed value of property, the average ratio of assessment to market value in different local jurisdictions varies widely. (4) State constitutions frequently place limits on property tax rates and on indebtedness of state or local governments based upon the assessed value of property. The common procedure of underassessment relative to market value unduly limits local tax revenues and debt potentials."

E. The Federal government can better guarantee a more equitable collection of funds for public elementary and secondary education.

1. The Federal tax structure is more progressive.

− Joseph Pechman (Brookings Institute) *Federal Tax Policy,* 1966, p. 50. "The individual income tax is uniquely suited for raising revenue in a democratic country where the distribution of income, and therefore of ability to pay, is unequal. Theoreticians may disagree about the meaningfulness of the term ability to pay, but the close association between a man's income and taxpaying ability is commonly accepted. There is also general acceptance of the idea of progression in income taxation.

The individual income tax has still another attractive feature. Income alone does not differentiate a man's ability to pay − his family responsibilities are also important. A single person may be able to get along on an income of $3,000 a year, but a married man with two children would have great difficulty making ends meet. The individual income tax takes such differences into account through the personal exemptions and deductions, which are subtracted before arriving at the income subject to tax."

− Ira Sharkansky (Professor of Political Science, Unviersity of Wisconsin) *The Politics of Taxing and Spending,* 1969, p. 14. "Of all the major taxes collected by the federal, state, and local government, the personal income tax of the Federal government is the only one that is progressive throughout the income ranges from (under $2,000 to $15,000 and over)."

— Otto Eckstein (Professor of Economics, Harvard University) *Public Finance,* 1967, pp. 14-15.
"We rely on the progressive Federal income tax to assure a fair distribution of the tax burden. It is our main policy instrument for reducing the inequality of the distribution of income in our society ... its impact is considerable . . . The nominal rate structure ranges from 14% to 70%."

— Ira Sharkansky (Professor of Political Science, University of Wisconsin), *The Politics of Taxing and Spending,* 1969, p. 15.
"The burden of all federal tax taxes tends to be progressive, reflecting the weight of the progressive personal income tax. In contrast total state and local taxes are regressive, reflecting the weight of sales, excise and property taxes."

2.   Intrinsically, the Federal tax structure is more equitable.

— *The American Almanac,* 1972, p. 379.
"Combined Federal individual normal tax and surtax rates by taxable income bracket:

| Taxable Income | 1970 (%) |
|---|---|
| $ 0 − 2,000 . . . . . . . . . . . . . . | 14 − 18 |
| 6 − 8,000 . . . . . . . . . . . . . . | 24 |
| 14 − 16,000 . . . . . . . . . . . . . . | 31 |
| 22 − 26,000 . . . . . . . . . . . . . . | 40 |
| 32 − 38,000 . . . . . . . . . . . . . . | 50 |

III. EQUITABLE FUNDING OF PUBLIC ELEMENTARY AND SECONDARY EDUCATION REQUIRES EXCLUSIVE FEDERAL DISTRIBUTION.

A.  State and local governments are unable to distribute funds equitably.

    1.  State distribution is inequitable on an interstate basis.

        — James W. Guthrie (University of California) *Equal Educational Opportunity,* Hearings, Select Committee on Equal Educational Opportunity of the United States Senate, 91st Congress, 2nd Session, Part 7, "Inequality of Economic Resources," September 30; October 1, 6, 1970, p. 3406.

        "One of our principal educational inequities occurs as a consequence of a child having the misfortune to reside in a relatively poor state. The disparity in resources spent on children in low wealth states, compared to those in high wealth states, is well known. . . . My point here is that such disparities are not simply a consequence of neglect or lack of concern on the part of the inhabitants of low expenditure states. On the contrary, in 1969, Mississippi residents taxed themselves at a rate equal to 4.42% of their personal income. Despite this level of effort they were able to generate an average of only $462 per pupil. By contrast, New York State residents made slightly less effort (4.26%) and raised $1,306 per pupil in the process."

        — Henry M. Levin (Stanford University) *IBID.,* p. 3509.

        ". . . At each level of government the amount of wealth or income of the population is the principal determinant of how much will be spent on the schooling of each student. Students who live in poorer jurisdictions havyless public funds invested in their educational development than students who live in wealthier areas. This means that on the average lower social class children will receive poorer schooling than middle class ones because there are higher concentrations of the poor children within the lower income jurisdictions.

    The average child in relatively low income Mississippi had about $476 spent on his education in 1969-70; while the average student in the wealthier state of Michigan received an educational investment of $842 and a student who resided in New Jersey had $963 spent on his schooling. These figures are representative of the disparities that exist in our Federal system. What is significant about this particular comparison is that all three states were making the same relative efforts spending about 4.7% of their incomes on education. Yet, with the same relative sacrifice the children in the latter two states received twice as many educational dollars as students in the former. At the extremes of the expenditure spectrum students in New York benefited from three times the educational investment of the average pupil in Alabama. To reiterate, these expenditures differences can be explained principally by differences in wealth, not effort. States that were trying equally hard showed vastly disparate results."

2. State and local distribution is inequitable on an intrastate basis.

    a.    Funds are not distributed equitably between rich and poor school districts.

        — Oliver Goldman, *Equal Educational Opportunity — 1971,* Hearings, Select Committee on Equal Educational Opportunity of the United States Senate, 92nd Congress, 1st Session, Part 16B, "Inequality in School Finance," September-October, 1971, p. 6754. "Unequal distribution of property tax resources exists among the separate taxing jurisdictions within metropolitan areas, the jurisdictions within a state, and among the states. Examples of distributional extremes were presented in a recent study done for the Federal Reserve Bank of Boston. In one state there exist two districts which have the same school tax rates, but one is spending three times as much per pupil as the other. In another instance two districts are spending the same amount per pupil, but one is levying school taxes at seven times the rate of the other. The property tax continues to be the backbone of public school finance and provides over one-half the revenue used to finance public schools in most of the United States today. Inequalities in the distribution of the property tax base, that is inequalities in the distribution of wealth among jurisdictions, accounts for a significant part of the unequal distribution of spending on schools."

        — James Guthrie, (University of California) op. cit., p. 3406. "As great as the school expenditure levels are among states, differences within states are even greater. For instance, in 1967 the range of school expenditures in California was $1,710 to $274. In Michigan, the comparable figures were $915 to $394. Moreover, as I described near the beginning of this paper, we are now coming to see that there is a wide range of resources spent on children within a school district. It is difficult to argue that each additional dollar spent for a child's schooling translates directly into an additional increment in achievement. Nevertheless, it is quite reasonable to assume that expenditure differences of the magnitude just listed are indeed associated with wide variations in the quality of schooling available to children."

74

– Paul D. Cooper, "State Takeover of Education Financing."' *National Tax Journal* (V. XXIV, 1971), p. 343.

"Examination of the revenue data (corresponds roughly to expenditures) reveals that total operation revenues from state and local sources varied from a low of $524 per pupil to a high of $789 per pupil – a ratio of 1 to 1.5. The state percentage share for the lowest expenditure county is 65.4% compared to 23.8% for the highest expenditure county. While considerable equalization is obviously being achieved, it appears that to some degree, the level of education expenditure depends upon the wealth of the district. Funds available from state and local sources are not revealed to be precisely in inverse ratio to per pupil wealth, but such is the tendency; and it may be significant to note that the highest and the lowest expenditure units have respectively the highest and lowest wealth.

. . . it will be questioned whether or not the districts with the least wealth are taxing themselves as heavily as the wealthier. . . . they generally are not. The district with the lowest expenditure and least wealth taxed itself only to the extent of 1.39% of its wealth as opposed to 1.67% for the district of greatest wealth and highest expenditure level. However other data presented indicates that the equal effort would by no means have resolved the disparities. The yield from a tax rate in each district equal to the highest imposed in any district is shown. If this yield is combined with the state aid for that year, it is found that the highest expenditure county would have had available a total of $945 per pupil as opposed to $616 in the lowest expenditure county. Stated another way, the poorest county, after state aid, would have had to tax itself 2.2 times as heavily as the wealthiest county to achieve the same expenditure level."

b.  Funds are not distributed equitably between inner city and suburban schools.

– John Shannon, (Assistant Director, Advisory Commission on Intergovernmental Relations) *Equal Educational Opportunity,* Hearings, Select Committee on Equal Educational Opportunity of the United States Senate, 91st Congress, 2nd Session, Part 7, "Inequality of Economic Resources," September 30; October 1, 6, 1970, p. 3551.

". . . our Commission has clearly documented the fact that with each passing year since 1957, the central city school districts are falling further behind their suburban neighbors. In 1957, the per pupil expenditures in the 37 metropolitan areas favored the central city slightly – $312 to $303 for the suburban jurisdictions. By 1965, the suburban jurisdictions had forged far ahead $573 to $499 for the central cities. This growing disparity between the central city and suburban school districts takes on a more ominous characte;in light of the fact that the central city school districts must carry a proportionately heavy share of the educational burden – the task of educating an increasing number of high cost underprivileged children. Children who need education the most are receiving the least."

– "Inequalities of School Finance," *Saturday Review,* January 11, 1969, p. 44.

"Despite the obvious need for more resources in city schools, we are spending less – any way you measure it – in the cities than in the suburbs. For the 37 largest U.S. metropolitan areas, the average per capita expenditure for education in the central cities is $82; the same expenditure in the suburbs is $113. On a per student basis, the comparable figures are $449 for the cities and $573 for the suburbs. These figures would not be so startling if the gap between city and suburb appeared to be closing. It is widening however. To compete with the suburbs, central cities must have a resource advantage. Yet the present system of resource allocation clearly discriminates against the city."

– *Report of the National Advisory Commission on Civil Disorders,* 1968; p. 434.

"Twenty-five school boards in communities surrounding Detroit spent up to $500 more per pupil per year to educate their children than the city. Merely to bring the teacher/pupil ratio in Detroit in line with the state average would require an additional 16,650 teachers at an annual cost of approximately $13 million."

3.  The limited jurisdiction of state governments precludes an equitable distribution of funds on an interstate basis.

– John F. Due (University of Illinois) *Government Finance: Economics of the Public Sector,* 1968, pp. 317-318.

"Higher levels of education promote more stable and effective political processes . . .; they bring more rapid technological change and economic growth, and higher levels of per capita real income. These benefits extend to the country as a whole, not merely to the particular school district or area. Secondly, persons are highly mobile . . .; persons educated in one area migrate to others, which benefit from the education. This effect is illustrated by the migration of large numbers of poorly educated persons from southern states to northern cities in recent years, bringing too the many problems that would have been avoided if the migrants had been better educated. . . . When some benefits are external, the level of activity is likely to be too small relative to the interests of the country as a whole, if the activity is financed locally and decisions about quantity to produce is left in local hands. . . . Equivalent spillings from governmental activities of other jurisdictions will not bring adjustment of expenditure to the optimum. . .”

— Terry Sanford (forme;governor of North Carolina) *Storm Over the States,* 1967, pp. 22-23.
"Our people flee to the city, and from there to the suburb, and they shuttle from city to city and state to state. Their migratory habits scatter the social problems of each region throughout the nationa. This movement, it is argued, converts local problems into national problems. Certainly it stimulates the demand for national action. Illinois has a stake in the kind of education its immigrating Negroes have received. California absorbs, for better or worse, the education brought by 33,000 new citizens who move there every month. Some of them dropped out in the fourth grade, but many of them have degrees from great Midwestern universities. How can one state insist that another state improve educational standards?How can one state afford to provide higher education for those who, upon graduation, go to other states to live and produce wealth?"

4. Political, economic and social forces preclude an equitable distribution of funds on an intrastate basis.

   a. State school aid formula's are inadequate.

      — "Inequities of School Finance," *Saturday Review,* January 11, 1969, p. 48.
      "State education formulas provide substantially greater aid to suburban districts than to city districts. . . . per capita education aid in the central cities was $20.73, while in the suburban areas it was $37.66. On a per student basis the gap is equally dramatic, as shown by data for New York state. In New York state's six metropolitan areas during the school year 1966-67, the average difference between educational aid to the central cities and that to the school districts in the rest of the counties in which the central cities were located was more than $100 per pupil."

      — Henry M. Levin, (Associate Professor, School of Education, Stanford) *Equal Educational Opportunity,* Hearings, Select Committee on Equal Educational Opportunity of the United States

Senate, 91st Congress, 2nd Session, Part 7, "Inequality of Economic Resources," September 30; October 1, 6, 1970, p. 3614.

"How do the states reconcile the unequal financial status of local districts for providing educational services under what is legally a state system of schools? The answer is rather straightforward. While the states provide some direct aid to local school districts, differences in ability are by no means reconciled. Indeed, the state aid arrangements are termed as equalization plans, a flagrant misnomer when one considers the effect of such plans. No matter what set of equilization arrangements the states have adopted, the arrangements seem to have two effects: On the average, the richer the school district, the greater will be the expenditures on each student, and the lower will be the tax burden as a proportion of wealth (or income). In fact there is evidence that many cities receive fewer dollars from the state for each pupil than do their wealthier suburbs. Though some states provide additional financial support to their cities for educating children from low income families, the supplemental aid is so nominal that the pattern does not change."

– Report of the Advisory Commission on Intergovernmental Relation, April, 1969, p. 47.

"Even where equalization governs the distribution of a large portion of state education assistance, such formulas may be based only in part on local ability, with additional measures also used. These additional factors may, in fact turn out to work against equalization. The Massachusetts distribution formula reflects these competing objectives. Under this approach, each locality receives an amount equal to the school aid percentage (where local ability is reflected) times the reimbursable expenditures – which, with some exceptions, are local expenditures from their own sources. Since it is the wealthy communities that then to undertake the greater expenditure from their own resources however, this part of the overall formula tends to offset the equalization effect. Thus wile one part of the formula favors the disadvantaged cities or towns, encompassing as it does the equalization feature, the second part reflects state aid based on the concept of reward for local initiative, which has the effect of favoring the wealthy communities."

– *IBID.,* p. 47.

"There are however, many points where slippage between the goal of equalization and the actual distribution of state aid may occur. In some states, for example, equalization relates to a relatively small portion of total state funds provided. Thus, while this portion may equalize – in the sense that a given amount of state aid is distributed so as to offset variations in local wealth — the amounts of such equalization aid may be relatively small and thus will have a lesser impact in terms of actual amounts received by localities. To put this point somewhat differently, while a portion of state aid may equalize, it may have only a slight impact on local service levels if the total funds for this purpose are small, while the totality of state education aid may, in fact, work against equalization."

*— IBID.*, p. 48.

"A final instance where the equalization objective might be thwarted are save harmless clauses which guarantee that no locality will receive less under the equalization than they had obtained in some previous year under an alternative distribution formula. A similar type provision is to establish a minimum figure of State aid for each locality regardless of what the equalization formula would have yielded. Where such provisions are in effect, the equalization tendency is constrained and the impact of such State aid is therefore reduced."

b.   State foundation programs are insufficient to provide for equitable distribution.

*— Equal Educational Opportunity—1971,* Hearings, Select Committee on Equal Educational Opportunity of the United States Senate, 92nd Congress, 1st Session, Part 16D-3, "Inequality in School Finance," Sept—Oct, 1971, p. 8288. "State systems of education finance distribute state funds through foundation programs which fail to correct the wealth disparities among local districts. While these programs vary widely in specifics from state to state they frequently suffer from three major flaws, and hose of minor ones: Foundation mounts — the maximum amount the state assures each district — are inadequate. For instance, California's maximum amount is $355 per elementary pupil, Maryland's is $370; Flat or minimum grants which award money on the basis of number of pupils to all districts, wealthy or poor. When they are awarded as part of the maximum foundation amount, as in California, or are substituted for districts not qualifying for minimum amounts under an equalization program, as in Maryland, they subsidize the wealthy and attenuate the disparities. Districts must raise money locally to support education programs superior to those provided for in the foundation amount. This gives rise to disparities in tax effort and in expenditures. Even though poorer districts make the same or greater tax effort on behalf of their schools, they are able to purchase much less education than the rich.

c.   Municipal overburden precludes equitable distribution of funds on an intrastate basis.

– Robert A. Dentler, (Director, Center for Urban Education, New) "Urban Education trends in the Seventies." *Needs of Elementary and Secondary Education for the Seventies,* General Subcommittee on Education, Committee on Education and Labor, House of Rep., 91st Congress, 1st Session, March 1970, p. 159.

"Less than one half of 1% of the more than 20,000 public school systems in the United States are currently responsible for educating more than one in five of the nations' systems, all of them urban, enroll more than one in three of the nation's students.

The city and large suburban populations served by the 400 largest school districts are declining only slightly in size while they continue to change rapidly in class and ethnic composition. As a result, the elementary and secondary public school populations of American urban communities will decline very slightly in the number of pupils enrolled during the 1970's, while the adult populations will continue to become poorer economically and ethnically more isolated."

– John Shannon, (Assistant Director, Advisory Commission on Intergovernmental Relations) *Equal Educational Opportunity,* Hearings, Select Committee on Equal Educational Opportunity of the United States Senate, 91st Congress, 2nd Session, Part 7, "Inequality of Economic Resources," Sept 30; Oct. 1, 6, 1970, p. 3557.

"The truth of the matter is that a small suburban school district and a large central city district may have tax bases with approximately the same amount of taxable property behind each student, yet because of the phenomenon of municipal overburden the central city school district would not be able to allow nearly as much per student for school purposes as the suburban district. Municipal overburden stems from the fact that central cities are forced to pay more per capita than their suburban neighbors for almost all public services – police, fire, sanitation and public health services."

– *IBID.,* p. 3551–2

"Our most recent reading of metropolitan disparities, based on 1967 data, indicated that 33.5 cents of each central city tax dollar went to education, while out in suburbia, 56 cents of each tax dollar was used for this purpose. Central city residents, more than their suburban neighbors, require more custodial type services – the demands of law and order and proverty related services are reflected in extremely heavy central city outlays for police, fire, sanitation, and other public services. Thus, about 66% of all central city expenditures go for; noneducational programs, while suburban communities devote 44% of their expenditures for noneducational purposes."

– Henry M. Levin (Assistant prof. School of Education, Stanford), *IBID*., p. 3614.
"Given the high contrations of students who need such assistance in the cities, the direct result is a greater financial burden for the city schools than for suburban ones. In summary, greater pupil needs, higher costs, municipal overburden, and smaller resources to draw upon means that the present system of financing the schools places the city at a severe disadvantage relative to the suburbs. It is more difficult for the city to raise equal dollars, equal dollars do not buy equal educational services because of higher costs in the city, and the educational services that the city must provide are far more massive than those that must be provided by suburban neighbors."

– *IBID*., p. 3509.
"...virtually all of the states claim to provide equalization aid. Another paradox rears its mysterious head until one examines the forms and amount of such aid. In most states even the richest districts receive financial assistance that amount to substantial portions of that received by poorer ones. Even so, the total amount of state aid is usually so low relative to expenditure levels that even so called equalizing funds make barely a dent in the vastly unequal pattern that mirrors the underlying disparities in local tax bases. Neither differences in local priorities nor in local efforts explain the enormous differences in educational expenditures within states. Rather, educational opportunity as reflected in school expenditures are determined primarily by variations in wealth. In other words the poor get less."

d.  The unresponsive nature of the state and local political system precludes equitable distribution.

– Marilyn Gittell (prof of pol. sci., and director, Institute for Community Studies, Queens College), "Educational Goals and School Reforms" *Needs of Elementary and Secondary Education for the Seventies*, General Subcommittee on Education, Committee on Education and Labor, House of Rep., 91st Congress, 1st Session, March 1970, -. 293.
"Most of the States have virtually ignored the special needs of education in the urban centers and inner cities. In their own

structures, they have yet to organize special urban education sections or to employ urban specialists. Grant in aid formulas, traditionally show little respect for the needs of the cities and their education problems. In fact, in many of the States there is an obvious antiurban orientation which acts to the detriment of city school systems and their school populations."

— Jack Witkowsky (former, member, Chicago Board of Education) "Education of a School Board Member," *Saturday Review* November 20, 1971. p. 92.

"The board had only a few standing committees, and even fewer of them exercised much power. . . .There was a regular opportunity at board meetings for committee reports, but only after the superintendant's agenda. Seldom did anything significant come out of the committee reports. The general public had an opportunity to address the board only twice a year, during hearings on general policy and the budget. The board consistently refused to let the public discuss current problems during its regular meetings. Friedman, an independent, was appointed chairman of a committee to study board procedures, but when he began to suggest giving the public greater opportunity to speak up, Whiston removed him from the committee and replaced him with Mrs. Wild, one of his most ardent supporters."

— *IBID.,* p. 92.

"Each teacher reported to a principal, who reported to a district superintendent, who reported to an area superintendent, who reported to the deputy superintendent, who reported to the general superintendent. . . .In all, the board had 40,000 employees. In organizations of this size buck-passing becomes a way of life. When a community demands action, low level employees frequently pass the buck on up the line until it reaches someone so remote that he cannot be subjected to community pressure."

— "Inequities of School Finance," *Saturday Review,* Jan. 11, 1969, p. 74.

". . .the behavior of city school boards does not indicate any sweeping changes in the allocation of resources. Nor is there much evidence that states are likely to provide greater assistance for their cities. The states have the power to assume functions which are performed locally. They could adapt their aid systems to current metropolitan patterns, and they could adjust the boundaries of local government accordingly. However, these powers and responsibilities have been exercised sparingly, if at all. The former bias in favor of suburban areas."

B.  Current Federal Aid programs are inadequate to provide for an equitable distribution of funds.

1.  Federal aid is negligible in impact.

   a.  The Declining amount of Federal aid is insufficient to offset inequitable state distribution.

      − "Federal Shares of School Expense at 6 year low," *The New York Times,* Jan. 12, 1971, p. 1.
      "The National Education Association reported today that it would cost a record total of $42.4 billion in 1970−71 to run the nation's public schools but that the Federal Government's share would drop to its lowest percentage level in six years.

      The NEA's 20th annual report of estimates of school statistics added that the failure of the Federal Government to pay a greater share of the cost of educating the nation's elementary 45 million elementary and secondary pupils would fall on financially pressed state and local governments.

      The Federal contribution reached 8% of the school dollar in 1967−68, but has dropped the last two years. The NEA estimated that Federal money would be only 6.9% of the total this school year. The lowest recent rate was 3.8% in 1964−65."

      − James Guthrie (Stanford Univ.) *Equal Educational Opportunity,* Hearings, Select Committee on Equal Educational Opportunity of the United States Senate, 91st Congress, 2nd Session, Part 7, "Inequality of Economic Resources," Sept 30; Oct 1, 6, 1970, p. 3404.
      "It is particularly ineffective in cities where the problems are the greatest. Moreover, the difficulty is compounded by the fact that federal funds do not flow in a proportionate fashion to big city districts. In fact, in a recent analysis in Michigan, it was revealed that the federal funds redistributed by the state actually exhibit a negative correlation with the social class of the child. That is despite the intent of Congress, federal funds flow disproportionately to districts serving wealthier students."

      − "Report of the Commissioners Ad Hoc Group on School Finance," *Equal Educational Opportunity−1971,* Hearings, Select Committee on Equal Educational Opportunity of the United States Senate, 92nd Congress, 1st Session, Part 16D−3, "Inequality in School Finance," Sept−Oct 1971, p. 8391.
      "The effect of the leveling and decline of federal aid is exemplified

by it operations on Title I. In 1968–69 school year, cutbacks of $68 million combined with the growing costs of education resulted in $400 million less for disadvantaged pupils in the local that year than was available in the first year of the program. In addition, the growth in the number of eligible pupils–both because of changes in the federal eligibility formulas and because many cities have experienced marked increases in the number of AFDC pupils – has made for a sharp decline in funds per poverty eligible pupil had declined to little more than half, from $365.64 to $200.10 in the four years of Title I operation."

– "Inequities of School Finance," *Saturday Review,* Jan 11, 1969, p. 74.
". . .today, the aid system does not allocate resources relative to need, whether measured as total need or for education alone. Most revealing about the present fiscal system is the failure of aid, either state or federal, to fill the gap left by the unequal distribution of local resources available. For example, state and federal aid supports 27% of public expenditures in central cities, while supporting 29% of those in suburban areas, and 37% of all local expenditures in the rest of the nation. . . .federal and state aid represents only 44% of the central city taxes; the comparable figure for suburbia is 53% and for the rest of the nation 74%."

b.  Current Federal aid formulas are inadequate in providing for equitable distribution.

"Report of the Commissioners Ad Hoc Group on School Finance," *Equal Educational Opportunity–1971,* Hearings, Select Committee on Equal Educational Opportunity of the United States Senate, 92nd Congress, 1st Session, Part 16D-3, "Inequality in School Finance," Sept.–Oct., 1971 p. 8392.
"Not only is federal support declining and fluctuating but it is also not channelling educational resources to where the needs are greatest – or offsetting the inequities of state and local finance patterns. One of the most consistent patterns of impact is that school districts in non-metropolitan areas, largely rural and school town in character, get more federal aid than do metropolitan areas. In California, Texas, and Michigan non-metropolitan areas receive an average 50% more aid per pupil than do the metropolitan areas.

Examination of aid distribution within metropolitan areas – between central cities and suburbs reveals that federal aid is insufficient to overcome the suburban advantage in locally raised revenues and state aid.

In short, federal aid has done little to close the wide gap in revenues available to education between high cost cities and their suburbs."

*— IBID.*, p. 8393.
"Federal aid is also not very effective in enhancing an equitable distribution on a number of other indicators. The SURC study defined equity in terms of the relationship of federal aid to some rough measures of economic, social, educational and fiscal need. The findings indicate that:
1) Federal aid tends to be mildly equalizing, but that within some metropolitan areas a distinctly dis-equalizing phenomenon exists.
2) The degree of equalization is usually too small to offset pre-existing disparities among school districts.
3) A number of individual federal programs operate to help rich districts get richer."

— James Guthrie (Stanford Univ.), "Educational inequality, School finance, and a plan for the '70's." *Equal Educational Opportunity,* Hearings, Select Committee on Equal Educational Opportunity of the United States Senate, 91st Congress, 2nd Session, Part 7, Sept. 30; Oct. 1, 6 1970, p. 3467.
"In 1967, federal appropriations accounted for almost 8% of all public elementary and secondary education expenditures for the entire United States. If distributed in an equalizing fashion, such an amount could substantially ameliorate revenue inequalities. However, such is not the case. The relationship in Michigan between school district AV/PP and receipt of federal funds is positive. That is, wealthier school districts tend to receive more federal dollars per pupil than do poorer districts."

*— IBID.*, p. 3468.
"Federal funds flow into a state under a wide variety of legislative authorities. It is true that ESEA Title I funds must redistributed by a state in accord with the number of children in a district whose parents' annual income is less than $2,000. However, ESEA Title I is but one authority. As examples to the contrary, in Public Law 815 and 874, the National Defense Education, the Education Professions Development Act, and a number of ESEA Title, no such equalizing contraint is in operation. Consequently, in general federal funds flow in a fashion which permits high SES and wealth (high AV/PP — Average expenditure per pupil) districts to receive as much or more federal money per pupil than low SES and poor (low AV/PP) districts."

2. Federal aid relies on existing state and local distribution systems.

– William Henderson, Helen Cameron (Ohio State Univ.) *The Public Economy*, 1969, p. 337.
"Traditionally, federal grants have been passed directly to the states rather than to local governments. Thus state control of local action is not impaired, . . .The state is generally free to set up programs within the standards laid out in the federal proposals. Federal grants for a variety of programs have been tied to formula like allocations. As a result, federal grants have not been directed to equalizing state fiscal capacity. . . .The federal government, . . .has generally tried only to attain minimum national standards rather than equal state programs."

– Michael W. Kirst (Stanford Univ.) "Delivery Systems for Federal Systems for federal aid, to disadvantaged Children," Oct. 7, 1971, *Equal Educational Opportunity–1971*, Hearings, Select Committee on Equal Educational Opportunity of the United States Senate, 92nd Congress, 1st Session, Part 17, p. 8623.
"In following a Federal grant as it leaves Washington, through the states, down to the locals, when you get to the local level you find they have numerous sources of income. Some of the cities, like the Detroit schools, have over 100 sources of income, including bonds, property taxes, special taxes for handicapped childre, several categories of State aid, and numerous Federal categories.

As the number of income sources increases, the ability of any single Federal source to trace the impact of his contribution decreases. Under multipocketed budgeting, local administrators plan their programs and then review all their income sources – including Federal grants – to find the needed resources. This procedure promotes local priorities at the expense of Federal ones. Districts plan how to shift their flexible resources to other uses as categorical grants become available."

– H. Thomas James (Dean, School of Education, Stanford Univ.) "Interdepende and School Finance: The city, the state, and the nation," *Eleventh National Conference on School Finance* NEA, 1968, p. 10.
"(There are) 170 grant in aid programs in 21 different federal departments and agencies operating through 92,000 units of government throughout the 50 states."

3. Reliance on existing state and local distribution systems results in inequitable distribution of federal funds.

   a. Existing state–local distribution systems are reinforced.

      – "Unconditional Revenue Sharing as a Solution to Fiscal Imbalance," Bernard Herber (U. of Arizona) *The Quarterly Review of Economics and Business,* Autumn 1968.
      "It is significant to observe that even though unconditional grants may assure greater interstate and interlocal equality in per capita tax burdens, they do not assure a redistribution of real income within a state or locality in terms of actual quasi-national and nonnational public goods consumed. This result will be subject to the decision–making discretion of the lower levels of government regarding use of the unconditional funds. A national social objective for greater equality in income distribution thus could be distorted."

      – Marilyn Gittell (prof. of Pol. Sci., Director, Institute for Community Affairs, Queens College) "Educational Goals and School Reforms," *Needs of Elementary and Secondary Education for the Seventies,* General Subcommittee on Education, and Labor, House of Rep., 91st Congress, 1st Session, March 1970, p. 293.
      "The inadequacy of state education apparatus will most certainly undermine existing and new Federal programs and should be a top priority in any effort to achieve change in the overall structure of education."

   b. Existing State–Local distribution systems utilize federal aid for the disadvantaged for general school aid."

      – *Equal Educational Opportunity–1971,* Hearings, Select Committee on Equal Educational Opportunity of the United States Senate, 92 Congress, 1st Session, Part 17, "Delivery Systems for Federal systems for federal aid to disadvantaged children," Oct. 7, 1971, p. 8827.
      "Title I money is not to be used as general aid. To do so dilutes needed services to poor children and denies them crucial benefits under the Act. When Congress enacted ESEA, it entended that Title I would enable local school districts to provide services and programs which they were unable to provide to meet the special educational needs of educationally disadvantaged children. However, many school districts see this massive infusion of federal funds as an opportunity to improve their schools generally, to buy large amounts of equipment and supplies, and to construct buildings and additions to schools."

*— IBID.*, p. 8828.

The law specifies that Title I assistance should go to:

— Individual children, not entire school populations;

— Children who have one or more educational handicaps and who come from low income families, not all children in all proverty area schools;

— Programs that seek primarily to raise the educational attainment or skills of children, not exclusively to projects or services dealing with health, welfare, or recreational needs of poor children.

The use of Title I as general aid typically falls into four categories:

1.  Title I funds purchase services, equipment, and supplies that are made available to all schools in a district or all children in a school even though many children reached are ineligible for assistance.

2.  Title I funds are spread around throughout all poverty-area schools instead of focusing on those target areas with high concentrations of low income families.

3.  Title funds are not going to eligible children at all.

4.  Title I State administration funds support non-Title I operations of State departments of education."

*— IBID.*, p. 8829.

"HEW auditors found that three Georgia school districts were making Title I projects available to all schools in the system. Gwinett County had a mobile curriculum center costing $70,646 serving all schools. A $340,763 reading clinic served all schools in Muscogee County."

*— IBID.*, p. 8830.

"Attala County, Mississippi constructed two lagoons for sewage disposal costing $16,000 with Title I money and installed an intercom system costing $1,750.

In Oxford, Mississippi a curriculum materials center is located at a non-Title I school near a police station, reportedly for fear of burglary. Furthermore, the Title I coordinator in Oxford is principal of a non-Title I, white school."

*IBID.*, p.8835.

"In Fresno County, California, during fiscal years 1966, 1967 and 1968, several school districts transferred approximately $930,000 to the county superintendent to construct, equip and operate a county-wide instructional television system which benefitted not just educationally deprived children but all children in the county.

Part of this money was used to remodel a county owned building for a television studio, to purchase and install equipment and to operate the system."

c.  Existing state–local distribution systems utilize Federal aid in un-targeted schools.

    *– IBID.,* p. 8836.
"An HEW audit of Lousiana school districts covering Title I expenditures in fiscal year 1966, the first year of the program, found that 23 parishes loaned equipment costing $645,624 to schools that were ineligible to participate in Title I programs. The auditors noted that much of the loaned equipment was set in concrete or fastened to the plumbing. Much of the equipment had been at ineligible schools since its acquisition."

d.  Existing state-local distribution systems utilize federal aid for the disadvantaged for salary increases and administrative costs unrelated to specific programs.

    *– IBID.,* p. 8843.
". . .some state agencies have used Title I funds to enhance the state department of education and their general operations rather than to administer Title I.

    An HEW audit report dated October 27, 1967, states that the Louisiana State Department of Education used Title I administration to pay for costs not directly related to the program, obligation of services to be rendered after the end of the project, a duplicate payment and various other unallowable costs. The total costs question by the HEW audit agency for State Administration amounted to $68,296, of 43% of total the costs claimed by the state. . ."

C.  Exclusive Federal distribution would better enable more equitable funding of public elementary and secondary education.

    1.  Exclusive federal distribution would guarantee equitable funding on an interstate basis.

    *– The Federal Budget: Its Impact on the Economy* – fiscal 1970, The national independent conference board, p. 43.
"The net impact of Federal fiscal operations on each state may best be determined by relating Federal payments allocated to each state to revenues originating within that state. If the ratio of payments to

revenues is greater than one, this indicates net inflow of Federal funds, whereas a ratio of less than one indicates an initial net withdrawal of funds by the Federal government. ...the combined fiscal impact of Federal taxing and spending is generally consistent with a broad pattern of income redistribution from the wealthiest to the poorer states."

– Terry Sanford (former Governor, North Carolina) *Storm Over the States,* 1967, p. 89.
"The grants ...redistribute the wealth of the nation to some degree, into areas which need it most....The North Dakota tax commissioner explained: 'In North Dakota, over half of all state and local funds go fo education and yet we have a very high out migration of college graduates. Our best earning potential ends up paying income taxes in other states. We have no way to recover any benefit from our high investment in education other than through a federal grant system."

2.  Exclusive Federal distribution would guarantee more equitable funding on an intrastate basis.

    a.  Federal distribution would be better able to compensate municipal overburden.

        – Charles Adrian (U. of California) *Governing Our Fifty States and Their Communities* 1967, p. 3.
        "...policy innovation is most likely to come through the institutions of the federal government. (1) Many state constitutions restrict the scope, effectiveness, and adaptability of state and local action. These self imposed constitutional limitations make it difficult for many states to perform all of the service citizens require, ...(2) Congress is generally more oriented toward urban problems than are state legislatures, ...(3) A victory at the federal level is likely to mean that a new or expanded program will be applied throughout the nation – a more efficient approach to action than are time and effort consuming separate appeals to 50 state or hundreds of local governments."

        – Roscoe Martin (Syracuse U.) *The Cities and The Federal System,* 1965, -. 28.
        "...the nation is no longer dependent solely upon ineffective or recalcitrant states for the achievement of national policy. The states enjoy rights and powers, both through constitutional provision and through practice, which permit them to play as important a role in the governance of America as they wish to play. That some states do not conceive their role as an active and vigorous one is a matter of

state, not of national, decision. The states generally — though by no means all states, are recumbent. . ."

b.    The Federal government's higher degree of visibility enhances the possibility of equitable funding.

— Ira Sharkansky (prof of Pol. Sci., U. of Wisconsin) *The Politics of Taxing and Spending,* 1969, p. 26.
"Survey research finds that citizens are more likely to comprehend national issues and participate in national elections than state or local elections. Specialists in public administration report that the federal bureacracy is better paid, more professional and less troubled by patronage or graft than state or local agencies. And many federal programs are run with sufficient flexibility to permit experimentation and the transfer of experience that is claimed for state and local activities."

3.    Exclusive federal distribution is not contingent on state and local distribution systems.

— *IBID.,* p. 26.
"The federal government generally has the greatest control over its economic environment, whereas state and local governments are more likely to bend in the face of economic constraints. This factor is. . .why the federal agencies rather than states or localities, may assume. . .responsibilities for new services."

R. L. Johns (U. of Florida) "Toward Equity in School Finance," *American Education,* November, 1971, p. 5.
". . .irrespective of how the money is raised, the costs of educating some youngsters — a blind child, for example, or one who is economically disadvantaged — are a good deal more than for others. Significant variations also are to be found in the cost of providing particular kinds of education. For example, because of the equipment required and for other reasons, a vocational education course costs a school district appreciably more than a course in history.

So, given these variations in costs, equality of educational opportunity is affected not only by how the money is raised but how it is allocated."

IV. EFFECTIVE DISTRIBUTION OF FUNDS FOR PUBLIC ELEMENTARY AND SECONDARY EDUCATION REQUIRES EXCLUSIVE FEDERAL POLICY ADMINISTRATION.

A.  Policy administration is contingent on effective legislative policy formulation.

1.  Legislative formulation is necessary to promulgate the rules and procedures of policy administration.

– Committee for Economic Development, *Making Congress More Effective,* September, 1970, pp. 9-10.
"The formulation of public policy is a joint responsibility shared with the executive branch, but in the final analysis it is Congress that adopts (or rejects) legislation that determines the health of the economy, the national security, the character of life both urban and rural, the condition of the environment, and the levels of generational, racial and other group tensions. . .

The quality of management throughout the federal establishment depends heavily upon Congress. The nature of basic legislation, appropriations, and legislative oversight can either impair an agency's effectiveness or make successful operation possible. Congress exercises powers in fields far beyond policy determination. It decress organizational patterns, administrative standards, personnel arrangements, program priorities, and pay levels. The most able of executives cannot manage effectively without Congressional support."

2.  Legislative formulation is necessary to mediate conflict, assess imputs, and represent the public in policy administration.

– William Keefe and Morris Ogul (University of Pittsburg, *The American Legislative Process: Congress and the States,* 1968, pp. 12-13.
"In its broadest sense, American lawmaking consists of finding major and marginal compromises to ideas advanced for legislation. The sifting and sorting of proposals accompanies the search for compromise – in caucus, in committee, on the floor, in negotiations with the executive, in confrontation with interest groups. The detail of bills are filled in at many stages in the legislative process, though especially in committees. One can say that any proposal of consequence serves something of a probationary period; its ultimate fate depends on how well its advocates succeed in bringing additional supporters to its side. The task is not simply to beat the drums to excite one's followers but to neutralize outward and probably opponents and to convince the uncertain. . . .The process of gaining converts to an idea is a process of accomodation, compromise and bargaining.

b.  Legislative formulation provides for Legislative oversight to maintain a check on Administrative performance.

   *— IBID.,* pp. 429-30.
   "... legislation is regularly fashioned around such terms as the public interest, fair standards, and reasonable regulations. ... legislators...shift the burden of more precise definition to the bureaucrats who are confronted by concrete problems. Legislatures thus escape the problem of definition, but at the same time, create opportunities for the exercise of administrative discretion. Since such rule making involves heavy policy overtones... Formal legal recognition of such interest in Congress came as part of the Legislative reorganization act of 1946 which stipulated that each committee should exercise continuous watchfulness over the activities of those administrative units acting within the subject matter jurisdiction of that committee."

B.  Legislative policy formulation is based on the ability to effectively translate plans into programs.

   — Roger H. Davidson, (University of California), *The Role of the Congressman,* 1969, pp. 18-19.
   "The primary function of the political system...is to provide mechanisms for specifying and implementing the goals of the larger society....As a second and related task, the polity must find means of mobilizing the resources or facilities needed to realize the goals that are selected....The politys outputs are in the currency of power, in the concrete form of decisions or policies. ...The Legislature, in terms of this model, is primarily an institution that contributes to the attainment of goals by securing support and integrating conflict among members of the System."

   — Ira Sharkansky (University of Wisconsin) , *The Politics of Taxing and Spending,* 1968, p. 78.
   "...contained specialization enables...intensive specialization among participants, an ability to manage partisanship and other sources of conflict within decision making bodies, and the acceptance of specialists recommendations by other officials in government. These features permit a professional or technical style of decision. (On the House Ways and Means Committee and the Senate Appropriations Committee) theryis a prevailing norm of restrained partisanship. Thus the norm of technical competance and professionalism seem more prevalent than partisan infighting in committee deliberations."

C.  State governments are unable to effectively translate plans into programs.

   1.  Planning inputs are not effectively integrated into Legislative formulation.

a.  Budgetary planning is not centrally determined or coordinated.

> *– IBID.*, p. 92.
> "Whereas the President of the United States formulates his budget with the assistance of an expert bureau of the budget, headed by his personal appointee, several governors must share budget formulation with persons who are politically independent. In Florida, and West Virginia, the governor is chairman of a budgeting board that includes the separately elected secretary of state, comptroller, treasurer, attorney general, superintendent of public instruction, and commissioner of agriculture. In Mississippi, North Dakota and South Carolina the governor is chairman of a group containing separately elected administrative heads, plus the chairman of the legislatures finance committees and members of the legislature named by the presiding officers. The Governor of Indiana has only indirect access to the formulation of the budget. His appointee sits on a board with legislatures appointed by the presiding officers of the house and senate. In thirteen other states, the governor works with a chief budget officer who is either separately elected or chosen by the U.S. Civil Service Commission."

b.  State agencies are unable to effectively advocate program planning alternatives.

> *– IBID.*, p. 93.
> "In about half the states, the governors face restriction on their tenure. Seventeen states prohibit their governors from succeeding themselves in office, and six other states limit the governor to one reelection. This tenure barrier may limit the financial expertise that the governor can develop, and it restricts his power in bargaining with the legislature. . .A study of government in Illinois summed up the power of the governor with a crisp analogy: The budget document may be compared to a huge mountain, which is constantly being pushed higher by underground geologic convulsions. On the top of the mountain is a single man, blindfolded, seeking to reduce the height of the mountain by dislodging pebbles with a teaspoon; that man is the governor."

2.  State legislatures are are limited in their ability to promulgate rules and procedures for administration.

a.  State legislatures face constitutional limitations.

> – James McGreagor Burns and Jack Peltason, *Government by the People,* 1969, p. 647.

"...state constitutions are less charters of self-government than straitjackets on the living presented by the dead past. Today's majorities find it hard to get the government action they wish. For example, construction of the Delaware Bridge, linking Philadelphia with Camden, New Jersey, was delayed for five years because of restrictive clauses in the Pennsylvania constitution. For many years the Oregon legislature could not create a state college in Portland because the constitution forbade the founding of any new public institutions outside Marion County."

– *IBID.,* p. 657.
"In most of the states the constitution limits the legislature to a regular session or a fixed number of days, usually sixty. A few states halt payment of legislature's salaries after a specified period; only infrequently do they stay in session when their pay stops."

b.  State legislatures face structural limitations.

– Ira Sharkansky, *The Politics of Taxing and Spending,* 1969, p. 90.
"...financial institutions in Congress and the federal administration have developed the techniques of contained specialization to permit them to handle complex issues with minimum conflict. The states appear to be without such developments...At the federal level, strong legislative committees are central features of contained specialization. However, state legislatures are weakened by the lack of a viable seniority systems. ...Without a seniority system, state legislatures are unlikely to develop any financial expertise among their members.

– *IBID.,* p. 91.
"State legislatures are restricted further by the nature of the budgetary decisions they are allowed to make. Whereas the congress decides about expenditures separately from revenues...the constitutions of several states require that expenditures not exceed projected revenues."

c.  State legislatures face personal limitations.

– *IBID.,* p. 179.
"In a number of states, the personal interests of important legislators seem to be more important than the needs of prospective clients as criteria that govern the location of hospitals, universities, parks and new highways. Locations that are convenient for prospective clients increase the costs of transportation and cut down the number of

clients who actually use the facilities, and they may require the construction of additional facilities that are located on the basis of need. . . ."

3.  State governments do not consider policy in programmatic terms.

    *− IBID.,* p. 95.
    The simplistic decision
    "The simplistic decision criteria that are used by many state and local budget makers. . .provide little encouragement to those who would use budget process as the vehicle for program planning. . . The budget system in state and local governments is populated not by officials who elevate their own past decision to the status of principal decision criteria and who devise nonprogrammatic decision rule   in order to reduce deficits or distribute surpluses."

D.  The federal government is better able to translate plans into programs.

    − Executive office of the President, Office of Management and Budget. *The U.S. Budget in Brief, Fiscal Year 1972,* (January, 1971) pp. 55-6.
    "The President's transmission of his budget proposals to the Congress each year climaxes many months of planning and analysis throughout the executive branch. Formulation of the 1972 budget, which covers the fiscal year beginning July 1, 1971 and ending June 30, 1972 began in the spring of 1970. About 10 months later, in January, 1971, the budget was formally transmitted to Congress."

    *− IBID.,* p. 55.
    "Individual budgets are formulated by each agency, reviewed in detail by the Office of Management and Budget throughout the fall and early winter and then presented to the President. Overall fiscal policy problems − relating to total budget receipts and outlays − are also reviewed again. Thus, the budget process involves the consideration simultaneously of individual program levels, and total budget outlays and receipts appropriate to the needs of the economy. The budget submitted to Congress reflects both of these considerations."

    *− IBID.,* p. 56.
    "In the spring, each agency evaluates is programs, identifies policy issues, and makes budgetary projections, giving attention both to important modifications, reforms and innovations in its programs, and to alternative long range program plans. After review in the agency and by the Office of Management and Budget, preliminary plans are presented to the President for his consideration. At about the same time, the President receives projections of the conomic outlook and revenue estimates prepared jointly by the Treasury Department, the Council of Economic Advisers, and the Office of Management and Budget."

decentralization or community control on the one hand, . . .and locally elected school boards at the local level would protect the financial interests of school in poor neighborhoods."

— Graham S. Finney (Urban Affairs consultant, Philadelphia) *Equal Educational Opportunity.* Hearings, Senate Select Committee on Equal Educational Opportunity of the United States Senate, 91st Congress, 2nd Session, Part 2 Introduction, continued. May-July, 1970, p. 905.

"Accountability is the word now often used to describe this attempt to relate the person and the position, the individual and the responsibilities he is expected to assume. For the classroom teacher, a definition of accountability may embrace a responsibility to give reading instruction, to assure a student's safety while in the teacher's custody, and to maintain classroom decorum. For a superintendent, it may suggest final responsibility to establish and enforce reading and other standards in all classrooms, to implement state imposed rules and regulations, and to assure due process for all personnel. Boiled down, the principle of accountability suggests a general ability to know who is doing what in a school system and, with that as a start, how well they are doing it. It clearly implies a base line from which quality can be judged in order that high performing staff members can be distinguished from the lazy and ineffective ones."

— *IBID.,* p. 907.

"From this nation's founding, the private citizen has been connected to his government on a basis of consent and in a spirit of confidence. The issue behind decentralization is whether this concept of social contract can be maintained at a time when it has become badly frayed in the eyes of many Americans."

B.  Cooperative Federal, state, and local administration effectively translates plans into programs.

1.  Expertise is recognized at all levels of government.

— "Charles Adrian (University of California) "State and Local Government Participation in the Design and Administration of Intergovernmental Programs," *The Annals of the American Academy of Political and Social Science,* May 1965, p. 35.

". . .the important divisions within the federal system are along functional lines, with the functional specialist at one level sharing the values and goals of functional specialists at the other levels."

– Daniel J. Elazar, (Temple U.) *American Federalism: A View from the States,* 1966.

"Consequently many of the ostensibly Federal rules applied to the states are really federal in origin – shpaed by the associations of professionals serving the states and localities as well as the federal government, whose responsibility it is to implement the very same programs."

– *IBID.,* p. 151.

"The standards governing the construction of federal aid for highways are devised by the American Association of State Highway officials working in cooperation with the Bureau of Public Roads. Similarly, the National Education Association and the American Association of State Universities have major roles in shaping the rules for implementing the various federal educational aid programs. The same situation prevails in most of the major cooperative programs."

– Charles Adrian (U. of California), *State and Local Government,* 1967, p. 94.

"The list of federal supervisory controls is long. However, before reaching the easy conclusion that the Federal Government makes all the rules. . .it should be pointed out that the areas of federal control are relatively few and that it is not politically expedient for Congress or the Federal administration to seek to impose many. . .policy controls upon the states or their subdivisions. . .rules are not viewed with alarm by state and local administrators because the sense of professional standards agrees with the professional standards of the Federal employees with whom they deal. They therefore see themselves being involved in a cooperative venture to apply professional standards and do not feel coerced."

2. Specific state-local requirements are effectively represented in the formulation of programs.

– Daniel J. Elazar, (Temple U.) *American Federalism – A View from the States,* 1966, p. 144.

"Congress insures a place on key committees for representatives of states and even localities most seriously affected by the actions of those committees and their counterparts in bureaucracy. This has given the states an important line of access to national policy making."

– Harvey Mansfield (Columbia U.) "Functions of State and Local Governments," *The 50 States and Their Local Governments,* 1967, p. 106.

"The influrence of the states is also greatly enhanced by the ability of state officials and political leaders to infiltrate sometimes to enfeeble, and more often to bend to their interests or inclinations, the powers and agencies of the national government."

– Daniel J. Elazar, (Temple U.), *American Federalism – A View from the States,* 1966, p. 152.

"The state agencies often lobby in Washington for legislative changes and larger appropriations for their programs or for entirely new programs through their professional association. The present federal grant programs for improving library facilities beginning with the 195 7Rural Library Service Act, is largely the product of the efforts of the American Library Association pressed by the states, just as the interstate highway program was planned and promoted by the American Association of State Highway Officials."

– Charles Adrian (U. of California) *Annlas of the American Academy of Political and Social Science,* May 1965, p. 81.

"Shared decision making offers an opportunity for influence to flow upward as well as downwards. Public office-holders and bureaucrats at one level of government influence decision making at higher levels of government in different ways. First, . . .lobbying. Not only do individual states and populous cities and counties sometimes have their own lobbyists in Washington. . .but many special organizations permit various groups to lobby collectively.

The Council of State Governments speaks for many state positions in Washington. . . .The Council has spawned many organizations which in turn also lobby. For example the National Governor's Conference, The National Conference of Chief State School Officers, and the National Association of Attorneys General are important.

Second, and somewhat · related to the first, is the continuous interaction through common interests, and often a common political party, of office holders at all levels. . . .Governors are in frequent contact with congressmen and senators relative to legislation affecting their states. . . .

Third, persons in offices at higher levels of government are frequently sympathetic to the policy demands of lower levels of government and frequently carry to the office a set of experiences and policy preferences which they had accumulated at the lower office. Many a U.S. Senator or Congressman is a former governor or mayor, or has held some other state or local officee. . . .

Finally, one level of government influences policy at higher levels through imitation. Much of the domestic policy enacted by Congress reflects in part, at least, experiences in particular states which serve to pioneer legislation on the subject. . . ."

3.  The flexibility engendered by cooperative administration promtes efficiency in decision making.

    – *New State Ice Company vs. Liebman,* (285-U.S. 262, 1932) United States Supreme Court Justice Brandeis.
    ". . .it is one of the happy incidents of the federal system that a single courageous state may, if its citizens choose, serve as a laboratory; and try novel social and economic experiments without risk to the rest of the country."

    – Rosce Martin, (Syracuse U.) *The Cities and the Federal System,* 1965, pp. 40-41.
    "The federal system wherever found is experimental and inexact, whether as concept or as practice. . . .The federal system was designed to effect a marriage of centrality and diversity; because these concepts vary from time to time there can be nothing static about federalism. American. . .is an evolving arrangement for the division of powers and the distribution of responsibilities among governments of different levels. Far from being rigidly bound by philosophical or ideological conceptions, the federal system is a pragmatic scheme that not only permits, but also requires adjustments to meet the varying needs of changing times."

# BIBLIOGRAPHIC LISTING

## BOOKS

—Bailey and Mosher, *ESEA, The Office of Education Administers a Law* Syracuse University Press, (Syracuse, New York: 1968)

—Bowles, Samuel, *Planning Educational Systems for Edonomic Growth,* Harvard University Press (Cambridge, Massachusetts: 1969)

—Bendiner, Robert, *The Politics of Schools,* Harpers and Row, (New York: 1969)

—Center for the study of Public policy, *Education Voucher: A Report on Financing Elementary Education by Grants to Parents.* (Washington, D.C.; US Office of Economic Opportunity: 1970)

—Coleman, James, and Campbell, Ernest et. al., *Equality of Educational Opportunity* US Government Printing Office (Washington, D.C.: 1966)

—Committee for Economic Development, *Budgeting for National Objectives,* (New York: 1966)

—Committee for Economic Development, *Education for the Urban Disadvantaged,* McGraw Hill, (New York, N.Y.: March, 1971)

—Committee for Economic Development, *A Fiscal Program for a Balanced Federalism,* McGraw Hill, (New York, N.Y.: June, 1967)

—Committee for Economic Development, *Making Congress more Effective,* McGraw Hill (New York, N.Y.: 1970)

—Committee for Economic Development, *The Schools and the Challenge of Innovation,* McGraw Hill (New York, N.Y.: 1969)

—Coone John E., *Private Wealth and Public Education, Harvard University Press,* (Cambridge, Massachusetts: 1970)

—Due, John F., *Government Finance: Economics of the Public Sector,* Richard D. Irwin, Inc., (Homewood, Ill.: 1968)

—Dye, Thomas R., *Politics, Economics and the Public,* Rand McNally and Co., (Chicago: 1966)

—*Economic Report of the President,* U.S. Government Printing Office, Washington, D.C.: 1972)

—Ehlers, Henry, *Crucial Issues in Education,* Harpers and Row, (New York: 1969)

—Elazar, Daniel J. *American Federalism: A view from the States,* Thomas Y. Crowell Co. (New York: 1966)

—Executive Office of the President Office of Management and Budget, *The U.S. Budget in Brief, Fiscal Year 1972,* U.S. Government Printing Office, (Washington D.C.: 1971)

—*Federal Role in Education,* Congressional Quarterly Service, (Washington, D.C.: 1967)

—Garfinkel, Irwin, *Values and Efficiency in Financing Education,* (Madison, Wisconsin: 1970)

—Gauerke, Warren E. *The Theory and Practice of School Finance,* Rand McNally (Chicago: 1967)

—Heller, Walter W. *New Dimensions of Political Economy*, W. W. Norton and Company, Inc., (New York: 1967)

—Katzman, Martin T., *Political Economy of Urban Schools,* Harvard University Press, (Cambridge, Mass.: 1971)

—Keefe, William, *The American Legislative Process, Congress and the States,* Prentice-Hall, Inc., (Inglewood Cliffs, New Jersey: 1968)

—National Center for Educational Statistics, *Analysis of Financial Statistics of Local Public School Systems,* U.S. Government Printing Office, (Washington D.C.: 1970)

—National Center for Educational Statistics, *Statistics of Public Schools Fall, 1969,* U.S. Government Printing Office (Washington D.C.: 1970)

—NEA Committee on Educational Finance, *Fiscal Planning for Schools in Transition,* (Washington D.C.: 1969)

—NEA Committee on Educational Finance, *Interdependence in School Finance: The City-The State-The Nation,* (Washington D.C.: 1968)

—NEA Committee on Educational Finance, *The Challenge of Change in School Finance,* (Washington D.C.: 1967)

—NEA Committee on Educational Finance, *Trends in Financing Public Education,* (Washington, D.C.: 1965)

—National Educational Finance Project, v. 2, *Economic Factors Affecting the Financing of Education,* 1970.

—Netzer, Richard, *Economics of the Property Tax,* Brookings Institute (Washington D.C.: 1966)

—Orfield, Gary, *The Reconstruction of Southern Education,* John Wiley and Sons, (New York: 1969)

—Pechman, Joseph A., *Tax Policy,* Brookings Institute (Washington D.C.: 1966)

—Reagan, Michael D. *The Administration of Public Policy,* Scott, Foresman and Co., (Glennview: 1969)

—*Report of the National Advisory Commission on Civil Disorders,* (New York Times: 1968)

—Ribick, Thomas I., *Education and Poverty,* Brookings Institution, (Washington D.C.: 1968)

—Sharkansky, Ira, *Spending in the American States* Rand McNally (Chicago: 1968)

—Thurow, Lester C. (ed) *American Fiscal Policy,* Prentice-Hall Inc., (Englewood Cliffs, New Jersey: 1967)

—*Title I of ESEA: Is it Helping Poor Children,* (New York: NAACP Legal Defense and Education Fund, 1969)

—U.S. Department of Health, Education and Welfare, *Digest of Educational Statistics, 1968,* US Government Printing Office, (Washington D.C.: 1968)

—U.S. Department of Health, Education and Welfare, *Title II Elementary and Secondary Education Act of 1965 (Third Annual Report, Fiscal Year 1968)* U.S. Government Printing Office (Washington D.C.: 1971)

—Wilensky, Gali R. *State aid and Educational Opportunity,* Sage Publications (Beverly Hills, California: 1970)

–*Education Aid to Federally Impacted Areas–Public Law 874.* Hearings, Subcommittee on Education of the Committee on Labor and Public Welfare, United States Senate, 91st Congress, 2nd Session, April 28, 29, 1970. Y4.L11/2:Ed8/26.

–*Education Amendments of 1971.* Hearings, Subcommittee on Education of the Committee on Labor and Public Welfare, United States Senate, 92nd Congress, 1st Session, March 3, 1971. Y4.L11/2:Ed8/27/Pts. 1–5.

–*Comprehensive Child Development Act of 1971.* Joint Hearings, Subcommittee on Employment, Manpower and Poverty and the Subcommittee on Children and of the Committee on Labor and Public Welfare, United States Senate, 92nd Congress, May 13 and 20, 1970. Y4.L11/2:C43/2/pts. 1–3.

–*Higher Education Act of 1965.* Hearings, Subcommittee on Education of the Committee on Labor and Public Welfare, United States Senate, 89th Congress, 1st Session, March–June, 1965. Y4.L11/2:H53/pts. 1–3.

–*Indian Education.* Hearings, Special Subcommittee on Indian Education of the Committee on Labor and Public Welfare, United States, 90th Congress, 1st and 2nd Sessions, 1967-68. Y4.L11/2:In2/2/pts. 1–5.

–*Indian Education, 1969.* Hearings, Subcommittee on Indian Education of the Committee on Labor and Public Welfare, United States Senate, 91st Congress, 1st Session, Deb.–May, 1969. Y4.L11/2:In2/2/969/pts. 1 and 2.

–*Higher Education Amendments of 1970.* Hearings, Subcommittee on Education of the Committee on Labor and Public Welfare, United States Senate, 91st Congress, 2nd Session, Deb.–August, 1970. Y4.L11/2:H53/970/pts. 1–4.

–*Equal Educational Opportunity.* Hearings, Select Committee on Equal Educational Opportunity, United States Senate, 91st Congress, 2nd Session on Equal Educational Opportunity, Part 1A, "Equality of Educational Opportunity, An Introduction". April–May, 1970. Y4.Eq2/pt. 1A.

–*Equal Educational Opportunity.* Hearings, Select Committee on Equal Educational Opportunity, United States, 91st Congress, 2nd Session. Part 1B, Appendix, April–May, 1970. Y4.Eq2:Eq2/pt. 1B.

–*Equal Educational Opportunity.* Hearings, Select Committee on Equal Educational Opportunity of the United States Senate, 91st Congress, 2nd Session. Part 2, Introduction Continued. May–July, 1970. Y4.Eq2:Eq2/pt. 2.

–*Equal Educational Opportunity.* Hearings before the Select Committee on Equal Educational Opportunity of the United States Senate, 91st Congress, 2nd Session. Parts 3A, 3A, 3C, 3D, 3E-Desegregation Under Law, June–August, 1970. Y4.Eq2:Eq2/pts. 3A, 3B, 3C, 3D, 3E.

–*Equal Educational Opportunity.* Hearings, Select Committee on Equal Educational Opportunity of the United States Senate, 91st Congress, 2nd. Session. Part 4–Mexican American Education. August 18, 19, 20, and 21, 1970. Y4.Eq2:Eq2/pt. 4.

–*Equal Educational Opportunity.* Hearings, Select Committee on Equal Educational Opportunity of the United States Senate, 91st Congress, 2nd Session. Part 5, "DeFacto Segregation and Housing Discrimination," Aug. 25, 26, 27, Sept. 1, 1970. Y4.Eq2:Eq2/pt. 5.

–*Equal Educational Opportunity.* Hearings, Select Committee on Equal Educational Opportunity of the United States Senate, 91st Congress, 2nd Session. Part 6, "Racial Imbalance in Urban Schools," Sept. 15 and 22, 1970. Y4.Eq2:Eq2/pt. 6.

–*Equal Educational Opportunity.* Hearings, Select Committee on Equal Educational Opportunity of the United States Senate, 91st Congress, 2nd Session. Part 7, "Inequality of Economic Resources," Sept. 30; Oct. 1 and 6, 1970. Y4.Eq2:Eq2/Pt. 7.

–*Equal Educational Opportunity.* Hearings, Select Committee on Equal Educational Opportunities of the United States Senate, 91st Congress, 2nd Session, Part 8, "Equal Educational Opportunity for Puerto Rican Children," Nov. 23, 24 and 25, 1970. Y4.Eq2:Eq2/pt. 8.

–*Equal Educational Opportunity.* Hearings, Select Committee on Equal Educational Opportunity, 92nd Congress, 1st Session, Parts 9A and 9B, "San Francisco and Berkely, California–Appendix," March 3, 4, 5, and 6, 1971. Y4.Eq2:Eq2/pts. 9A and 9B.

–*Equal Educational Opportunity–1971.* Hearings, Select Committee on Equal Educational Opportunity of the United States Senate, 92nd Congress, 1st Session, Part 10, "Displacement and Present Status of Black School Principals in Desegregated School Districts," June 14, 1971. Y4.Eq2.Eq2/pt. 10.

–*Equal Educational Opportunity.* Hearings, Select Committee on Equal Educational Opportunity of the United States Senate, 92nd Congress, 1st Session, Part 11, "Status of School Desegregation Law," June 15, 1971, Y4.Eq2:Eq2/Pt. 11.

–*Equal Educational Opportunity–1971.* Hearings, Select Committee on Equal Educational Opportunity of the United States Senate, 92nd Congress, 1st Session, Part 12, "Compensatory Education and Other Alternatives in Urban Schools," July 14, 15; Aug. 3, 1971. YrEq2:Eq2/pt. 12.

–*Equal Educational Opportunity.* Hearings, Select Committee on Equal Educational Opportunity of the United States Senate, 92nd Congress, 1st Session, Part 13, "Quality and Control of Urban Schools," July 27, 29; Aug. 5, 1971. Y4.Eq2:Eq2/pt. 13.

–*Equal Educational Opportunity–1971.* Hearings, Select Committee on Equal Educational Opportunity of the United States Senate, 92nd Congress 1st Session, Part 14, "State Role in School Desegregation, Pennsylvania," Aug. 4, 1971. Y4.Eq2:Eq2/pt. 14.

–*Equal Educational Opportunity–1971.* Hearings, Select Committee on Equal Educational Opportunity of the United States Senate, 92nd Congress, 1st Session, Part 15, "Education in Rural America," Aug. 1971. Y4.Eq2:Eq2/pt. 15.

–*Equal Educational Opportunity–1971.* Hearings, Select Committee on Equal Educational Opportunity of the United States Senate, 92nd Congress, 1st Session, Parts 16A, 16B, 16D, 2 and 3, "Inequality in School Finance; Appendixes," Sept.–Oct., 1971. Y4.Eq2:Eq2/pts. 16A, 16B, 16D, 2 and 3.

–*Equal Educational Opportunity–1971.* Hearings, Select Committee on Equal Educational Opportunity of the United States Senate, 92nd Congress, 1st Session, Part 17, "Delivery Systems for Federal Aid to Disadvantaged Children," Oct. 7, 1971. Y4.Eq2:Eq2/pt. 17.

–*Equal Educational Opportunity–1971*. Hearings, Select Committee on Equal Educational Opportunity of the United States Senate, 92nd Congress, 1st Session, Part 18, "Pupil Transportation Costs," Oct. 6, 1971. Y4.Eq2:Eq2/pt. 18.

–*Equal Educational Opportunity–1971*. Hearings, Select Committee on Equal Educational Opportunity of the United States Senate, 92nd Congress, 1st Session, Part 19A, "Equal Educational Opportunity in Michigan," Oct. 26; Nov. 1 and 2, 1971. Yr.Eq2:Eq2/pt. 19A.

–*Equal Educational Opportunity–1971*. Hearings, Select Committee on Equal Educational Opportunity of the United States Senate, 92nd Congress, 1st Session, Part 20, "Unequal School Practices," Nov. 8, 1971. Y4.Eq2:Eq2/pt. 20.

–*Equal Educational Opportunity–1971*. Hearings, Select Committee on Equal Educational Opportunity of the United States Senate, 92nd Congress, 1st Session, Part 21, "Metropolitan Aspects of Educational Inequality," Nov. 22, 23, 30, 1971. Y4.Eq2:Eq2/pt. 21.

–*Needs of Elementary and Secondary Education for the Seventies–1971*. Hearings, General Subcommittee on Education of the Committee on Education and Labor, House of Rep., 92nd Congress, 1st Session, May 21, June 4, 1971. Y4.Ed8/1:Ed8/35/971.

–*Needs of Elementary and Secondary Education for the Seventies*. Hearings, Subcommittee on Education of the Committee on Education and Labor, House of Rep., 91st Congress, 1st Session, 2nd Session, Oct-Dec., 1969; March and April, 1970. Y4.Ed8/1:Ed8/35/pts. 1, 2, 3.

–*Higher Education Amendments of 1971*. Hearings, Special Subcommittee on Education of the Committee on Education and Labor, House of Rep., 92nd Congress, 1st Session, March, April and July, 1971. Y4.Ed8/1:Ed8/26/971/pts. 1 and 2.

–*Survey of Lender Practices Relating to the Guaranteed Student Loan Program established by the Higher Education Act of 1965*. Committee on Education and Labor, House of Rep., March 1970. Y4.Ed8/1:St9/4.

–*Student Financial Aid*. Hearings, Special Subcommittee on Education of the Committee on Education and Labor, House of Rep., 91st Congress, 1st Session, July 23, 24, 29 and 30, 1969. Y4.Ed8/1:St9/3.

–*Comprehensive Preschool Education and Child Day-Care Act of 1969*. Hearings, Select Subcommittee on Education of the Committee on Education and Labor, House of Rep., 91st Congress, 1st and 2nd Sessions, Nov.–Dec. 1969; Feb. and March, 1970. Y4.Ed8/1:P92/2.

–*Comprehensive Child Development Act of 1971*. Hearings, Select Subcommittee on Education of the Committee on Education and Labor, House of Rep., 92nd Congress, 1st Session, May 17, 21, and June 3, 1971. Y4.Ed8/1:C43/8.

–*Gifted and Talented Children Educational Assistance Act*. Hearings, General Subcommittee on Education of the Committee on Education and Labor, House of Rep., 91st Congress, 1st Session, July 15, 1969. Y4.Ed8/1:C43/6.

–*Vocational Education Amendments of 1969*. Hearings, General Subcommittee on Education of the Committee on Education and Labor, House of Rep., 91st Congress, 1st Session, Sept. 25, 1969. Y4.Ed8/1:V8 5/2/969.

—*Reports on the Implementation of the Vocational Education Amendments of 1968.* General Subcommittee on Education of the Committee on Education and Labor, House of Rep., Nov. 1971. Y4.Ed8/1:V85/2/968.

—*National School Lunch Act.* Hearings, Select Subcommittee on Education of the Committee on Education and Labor, House of Rep. 89th Congress, 2nd Session, July 21, 1966. Yr.Ed8/1:Sch6/25.

—*National School Lunch Program.* Hearings before Committee on Education and Labor, House of Rep. 91st Congress, 1st Session. March 6, 1969. Y4.Ed8/1:Sch6/26.

—*School Construction.* Hearings, General Subcommittee on Education of the Committee on Education and Labor, House of Rep. 91st Congress, 1st Session Feb. 25, May 6 and 8, 1969. Y4.Ed8/1:Sch6/23/969.

—*School Construction, 1965.* Hearings, General Subcommittee on Education of the Committee on Education and Labor, House of Rep., 89th Congress, 1st Session, July–Aug., 1965. Y4.Ed8/1:Sch/23.

—*Investigation of the Schools and Poverty in the District of Columbia.* Hearings before the Task Force on Anti-Poverty in the District of Columbia, of the Committee on Education and Labor, House of Rep., 89th Congress, 1st and 2nd Sessions, Oct, 1965; Jan. 1966. Y4.Ed8/1:Sch6/22.

—*Disaster School Assistance and Measures to Eliminate Inequities in Public Laws 815–874.* Hearings before the General Subcommittee on Education of the Committee on Education and Labor, House of Rep., 89th Congress, 1st Session, May 18, 19, 24 and 26, 1965. Y4.Ed8/1:Sch6/19.

—*Elementary and Secondary School Act Formulas.* Hearings before the General Subcommittee on Education of the Committee on Education and Labor, House of Rep., 89th Congress, 1st Session, July 16 and 22, 1965. Y4.Ed8/1:Sch6/21.

—*School Assistance to Federally Affected Areas.* Hearings, General Subcommittee on Education of the Committee on Education and Labor, House of Rep., 89th Congress, 1st Session, April 2, 3, 4, and 9, 1963. Y4.Ed8/1:Sch6/13/963.

—*To Amend the National School Lunch Act to Strengthen and Expand Food Service Programs.* Hearings, General Subcommittee on Education of the Committee on Education and Labor, House of Rep., 90th Congress, 2nd Session, Jan. 18 and 24, 1968. Y4.Ed8/1:N21s/2.

—*Extension of Elementary and Secondary Education Programs.* Hearings, Committee on Education and Labor, House of Rep., 91st Congress, 1st Session, Jan. Feb., March, 1969. Y4.Ed8/1:Ed8/34/pts. 1, 2, 3.

—*Departments of Labor, and Health, Education and Welfare Appropriations.* Fiscal Year, 1970. Senate Hearings, 91st Congress, 1st Session. Y4.Ap6/2:L11/970/pts. 1–7.

—*Departments of Labor, and Health, Education and Welfare Appropriations.* Fiscal Year, 1971, Senate Hearings, 91st Congress, 2nd Session. Y4.Ap6/2:L11/971/pts. 1–6.

—*Departments of Labor and Health, Education and Welfare and Related Agencies Appropriations.* Fiscal Year 1972, 92nd Congress, 1st Session, Y4.Ap6/2:L11/972/pts. 1–6.

—*Needs of Elementary and Secondary Education for the Seventies.* A Compendium of Policy Papers, Compiled by the General Subcommittee on Education of the Committee on Education and Labor, House of Rep., 91st Congress, 1st Session, March 1970. Y4.Ed8/1:Ed8/36.

—*Children with Learning Disabilities Act of 1969.* Hearings, General Subcommittee on Education of the Committee on Education and Labor, House of Rep., 91st Congress, 1st Session, July 8, 9, and 10, 1969. Y4.Ed8/1:C43/5.

—*Child Development Specialists.* Hearings, General Subcommittee on Education of the Committee on Education and Labor, House of Rep., 89th Congress, 1st Session, Oct. 19, 20, 1965. Y4.Ed8/1:Cre/3.

—*Aid to Elementary and Secondary Education.* Hearings, General Subcommittee on Education of the Committee on Education and Labor, House of Rep., 89th Congress, 1st Session, Jan—Feb. 1965. Y4Ed8/1:Ed8/24/pts. 1 and 2.

—*Elementary and Secondary Education Amendments of 1966.* Hearings, General Subcommittee on Education of the Committee on Education and Labor, House of Representatives, 90th Congress, 2nd Session, March 1966. Y4.Ed8/1:-Ed8/24/966/pts. 1 and 2.

—*Elementary and Secondary Education Amendments of 1967.* Hearings before the Committee on Education and Labor, House of Rep., 90th Congress, 1st Session, March 1967. Y4.Ed8/1:Ed8/24/967/pts. 1 and 2.

—*Extension of Elementary and Secondary Education Programs.* Hearings before the Committee on Education and Labor, House of Rep., 91st Congress, 1st Session, February—March, 1969. Y4.Ed8/1:Ed8/34/pt. 1—4.

—*Educational Technology Act of 1969.* Hearings, Select Subcommittee on Education of the Committee on Education and Labor, House of Rep., 91st Congress, 2nd Session, March 12, 1970. Y4.Ed8/1:Ed8/38.

—*Including Children of Refugees in Benefits of Impact Aid Legislation.* Hearings, Committee on Education and Labor, House of Rep., 91st Congress, 1st Session, Oct. 3, 1969. Y4.Ed8/1:C43/7.

—*Final Report-School Assistance in Federally Affected Areas—A Study of Public Laws 81—874 and 81—815.* Committee on Education and Labor, House of Rep., 91st Congress, 2nd Session, Dec., 1969. Y4.Ed8/1:Sch6/13/970.

—*Allocation of 1971 Appropriations to Education.* Hearings, Ad Hoc Sub-Committee on Oversight of Education Programs of the Committee on Education and Labor, House of Rep., 91st Congress, 2nd Session, Oct. 12, 1970. Y4.Ed8/1:Ed8/37.

—*Revenue Sharing and Its Alternatives: What Future for Fiscal Federalism?* Prepared for the Subcommittee on Fiscal Policy of the Joint Economic Committee, Congress of the United States, Volume I: Lessons of Experience — July, 1967. Y4.Ec7:-R32/2/v. 1.

—*Revenue Sharing and Its Alternatives: What Future for Fiscal Federalism?* Prepared for the Subcommittee on Fiscal Policy of the Joint Economic Committee, Congress of the United States, Volume II: Range of Alternatives for Fiscal Federalism. July 1967. Y4.Ec7:R32/2/v. 2.

*—Revenue Sharing and Its Alternatives: What Future for Fiscal Federalism?* Prepared for the Subcommittee on Fiscal Policy of the Joint Economic Committee, Congress of the United States, Volume III: Federal, State, Local Fiscal Projections, July 1967. Y4.Ec7:R32/2/v. 3.

*—Regional Planning Issues.* Hearings before the Subcommittee on Urban Affairs of the Joint Economic Committee, Congress of the United States, 91st Congress, 2nd Session, Oct. 13, 14, and 15, 1970. Y4.Ec7:P69/4/pt. 1.

*—Changing National Priorities.* Hearings, Subcommittee on Economy in Government of the Joint Economic Committee, Congress of the United States, 91st Congress, 2nd Session, June 1, 2, 4, and 5, 1970. Y4.Ec7:P93/10/pt. 1.

*—Proposed Fiscal Year 1972 Administration Budget for Programs Administered by the U.S. Office of Education.* Committee on Education and Labor, House of Rep., 92nd Congress, 1st Session, Deb., 1971. Y4.Ed8/1:B85.

*—A Compilation of Federal Education Laws.* Committee on Education and Labor, House of Representatives, October, 1971. Y4.Ed8/1:Ed8/33/971.

*—Meeting Parents Halfway: A Guide for Schools.* United States Department of Health, Education and Welfare, 1970. HE5. 220:20/64.

*—Focus on Innovation: ESEA Title III-FY 1969.* United States Department of Health, Education and Welfare, 1971. H #5. 220: 20/68.

*—Analysis of Financial Statistics of Local Public School Systems, 1967–68.* United States Department of Health, Education and Welfare, 1970. HE5. 220:20/67.

*—Statistics of Local Public School Systems, Fall 1969–Pupils and Staff.* United States Department of Health, Education and Welfare, 1971. HE5. 220:20/12-69.

*—Education of the Disadvantaged. An Evaluative Report on Title I, Elementary and Secondary Education Act of 1965–Fiscal Year 1968.* United States Department of Health, Education and Welfare, 1970. HE5. 237:37013-68.

*—Digest of Educational Statistics, 1968.* United States Department of Health Education and Welfare, 1968. HE5. 210: 10024-68.

*—The New Environmental Education Program.* United States Department of Health, Education and Welfare, 1971. HE5. 210: 10078.

*—Trends in Postsecondary Education.* United States Department of Health Education and Welfare, 1970. HE5.250:50063.

*—Follow Through–Promising Approaches to Early Childhood Education, School Year, 1970-71.* United States Department of Health Education and Welfare, 1971. HE5.220:20165.

## NEW YORK TIMES INDEX

### 1969

Ja  12 :  Influx of Puerto Rican and Southern Negro children places financial strain on school systems, 60:1

F    5 :  Calif. Teachers Assn. (NEA) imposes sanctions against Richmond Unified School Dist. for failing to provide adequate financing of its schools, 38:1

F   6 :   Educ. Comr. designate Allen says number 1 priority massive Fed. aid to urban educ., 1:1

MR  3 :   Danville, Ill. voters approve educ. tax rise, 1st in 22 yrs, 14:8

Je  5 :   Cabinet Educ. Subcom. outlines plan for radical rise in Fed. educ. support, 1:3

Jl  2 :   NEA study group urges Fed. Gvt. assume at least one third cost of funding ps. educ. in major cities, 48:3

Jl  9 :   Comr Allen predicts Fed Govt will triple its share of educ costs by 80's, 18:3

S   2 :   NY Times survey of 13 NY Met Area counties finds taxpayer revolts among issues marking reopening of school yr., 1:8

## 1970

Ja  1 :   Educ Comr Allen says his personal goal for '70 is to lead educ to top of domestic priorities within Nixon Adm., 20:4

Ja  4 :   10 Ohio School dists, closed during Nov and Dec because of lack of operating funds, reopen, 59:3

Ja  5 :   NEA rept finds Fed spending is $26 million less in '69–70 fiscal yr than for '68–69, 30:3

JA 11 :   Nixon Adm is expected to shift educ funds to programs which it believes are more needed than some others, 1:2

Ja 12 :   Charts on grade and hs expenditures; on educ expenditures as percent of GNP '30-68, 64:4

Ja 12 :   C I Foltz calls for greater Fed aid to meet educ needs of rural areas, 67:2

Ja 24 :   Senate comm recommends $35 billion educ bill, 18:4

Ja 25 :   Article discusses pros and cons of impacted aid program, 46:3

Ja 27 :   Pres Nixon vetoes appropriations bill, 1:8

Ja 27 :   Transcript of veto message, 24:1

Ja 28 :   Pres Nixon sends veto message to Cong explaining his action, 1:8

Ja 29 :   HR votes, 226-191 to sustain veto, 1:8

F   6 :   HR subcom drafts compromise appropriations bill calling for $700 million more than Nixon educ budget but about $550 million less than vetoed bill, 30:1

F   7 :   Sen Eagleton, sponsor of pub housing provision, admits impacted program is in disrepute but stresses educ benefits which can be afforded children in pub housing, 1:2

F  17 :   HR Appropriations Com passes amendment giving Pres Nixon discretionary power not to spend educ aid money appropriated by Cong. 1:1

F  18 :   Delegates at Amer School Admrs Assn conv say money and inflation are biggest problems facing schools and claim systems do not have enough money to meet rapidly expanding needs and costs, 24:4

F  20 :   HR approves $19.4 billion health and educ appropriations bill for current fiscal yr, 1:6

F 22 : NEW Dept Urban Educ Task Force recommends Fed Govt invest $470 Million in Urban schools in '71, 88:3

F 27 : Pres Nixon calls for elimination or change in impacted aid program, 14:1

Mr 4 : Pres Nixon says nation has no clear idea of which programs effectively aid poor children and calls for extensive re-examination of educ methods before making massive increases in educ aid, 1:1

Mr 19 : Los Angeles voters reject property tax increase plan which officials say is necessary to head off $47 million deficit, 26:4

Ap 2 : Sen passes $24.6 billion educ aid bill, extending aid program for 3 years and including over $1 billion for impace area schools, 1:6

Ap 14 : Nixon signs bill but criticizes it as unrealistically expensive 30:4

Ap 22 : Nixon discusses possible adverse affects of closing of private schools in terms of placing added burden on pub funds, 45:1

My 2 : Nixon signs bill providing up to $2.5 million in emergency funds for impacted areas, 31:3

My 5 : Los Angeles Educ Bd says it will cut 1 period from school day in all hss to help bridge $42 million deficit, 13:4

My 24 : HEW Dept survey covering 5 yr period finds voter approval of school bond issues dropped from 80% to 44%, 80:5

Jl 7 : NEA calls on Fed and State govts to withhold new aid and programs for private schools and to withdraw help such schools now receive from tax funds, 27:1

Jl 17 : HR passes compromise $4.4 billion educ appropriation bill for fiscal '71, 1:7

Ap 19 : Senate overrides veto completing enactment of measure, 1:8

A 14 : Dr. R L Johns holds educ financial crisis on communities will continue unless Fed and state govts share financial load, predicts Fed and state aid will cover 80% of school costs by '80, 1:3

O 13 : Nixon orders that only 91% of $4.4 billion educ aid appropriation be spent because of budget squeeze, 16:5

O 23 : HEW Dept Sec Richardson announces dept is releasing $387 million in educ funds that had previously been withheld as inflationary 46:4

N 8 : NY Times survey of statewide referendums finds voters across nation rejected school spending proposals in at least 10 states and defeated general taxing or const proposals relating to educ in several other states, 85:1

## 1971

Ja 11 : NY Times Special educ survey, PP. 47-48

JA 11 : Prelim. findings of Natl Educ Finance Project, 67:5

Ja 12 : NEA annual report on operating costs, 31:4

Ja 23 : Nixon's State of Union message, outlines $11 billion revenue sharing proposal, earmarked for 6 broad categories, including educ, 13:1

Ja 30 : Nixon's fiscal 72 budget message proposes consolidation of some sections of 65 Elementary and Secondary Educ Acts, 10:4

Ja 30 :  Analyses of budget shows aid to education in 72 to rise only 5%, 10:3

Ja 30 :  Graph shows growth of Fed aid to states from fiscal '61, 13:4

Ja 31 :  Rept on study by Policy Inst of Syracuse U. Research corp. on fed aid to urban and rural schools, 64:5

F   8 :  NY Times survey finds public and nonpub and colleges amont hardest hurt by economic crises, 26:1

F  11 :  Adm version of emergency desegregation bill would allocate 80% of funds to states on basis on minority pop., 58:1

F  17 :  AFL-CIO exec councils urges Congress to reject block grants for educ., 15:3

Mr  1 :  Census repts educ level of Spanish speaking population of 35 or older only 8.5 yrs., 24:1

Mr 15 :  Com for Econ Develop releases report on Educ for the Urban disadvantages, 1:6; 1:7

Mr 15 :  NY Times survey finds many school systems facing taxpayers revolt, 31:1

Mr 16 :  Sen Mondale accuses Nixon adm of improper handling of funds to ease desegregation, 1:7

Mr 25 :  Sen Educ Subcom approves compromise measure for desegregation aid, 23:1

Mr 19 :  NEA finds dramatic decline in no. of black teachers and principals in Southern communities, 1:7

Ap  7 :  Nixon outlines revenue sharing proposal for aid to educ, 1:8

Ap 21 :  Sup Ct upholds const. of busing, 1:8

My 19 :  Nixon says his educ revenue sharing proposal will greatly aid disadvantages children, 1:6

My 25 :  Budget cust in educ services seen key econ measure in nations cities, 1:1

My 30 :  Phil schools will reopen despite $20 mil deficit, 59:1

Je  4 :  Phil schools system, facing $100 million deficit, announces abolishment of varsity sports and nearly 2,000 jobs, 36:2

Je  6 :  HEW rept finds percentage of black students attending white schools rose last 2 yrs, 1:3

Je 18 :  HEW report on integration throughout the nation, 1:5

Je 18 :  Failure in present lunch program, 18:1

Jl  2 :  Voucher plan making slow progress in 6 districts across country, 14:1

Jl 12 :  Nixon signs record $5.15 billion educ bill, 1:1

Ag 28 :  NY Times survey finds increasing problem of mass expulsion of black students in South, 1:1

Ag 30 :  Figures show Fed lunch program failing to reach 1.9 mil needy children, 15:1

Ag 31 :  NY Times survey finds desegregation for first time outside of South and Border States, 1:7

Ag 31 :  Calif State Sup Ct rules that states system of financing pub Education is unconst., 23:2

S   1 :  Chief Justice Berger says lower cts are misreading recent Sup Ct ruling on busing, 1:1

S   1 :   Comr Marland says Calif Sp Ct decision may mean re-examination of current state formulas, 17:1
S  19 :   Nixon's Comm on School Finance calls nations property tax systems "hodgepodge", 45:1
S  22 :   Phil schools supt urges Fed Govt nationalize nations largest 25 urban school systems, 26:4
O   1 :   Leaders of 9 educ organizations urge Fed share of pub educ costs be increased from 8 to 40%, 21:6
O  31 :   Discussion of financial crisis in Ohio school districts IV, 12:1
N   3 :   Nat. Educ Finance Project finds great inequities in funding of schools, 53:1
D   3 :   Nixon pledges to seek reform of school financing, 46:3
D  14 :   NY Times survey on mounting money crisis, 1:4
D  17 :   U.S. educ comr holds Fed Govt should pay 25 to 30% of ps educ costs, 44:1
D  27 :   US Census Bur report shows black gains in education in past decade did not equal whites, 22:1


## 1972

Ja   7 :   Schultz says value added tax is one possibility as substitute for local property tax, 1:8
Ja   9 :   US Educ Office on 84 inner-city school systems, 59:1
Ja  10 :   NY Times annual educ review, XX, pp. 3-32


PERIODICALS
FEDERAL AID

1. "Acceptable compromise: health and education bill." New Repub 162:11 Mr 14 '70.
2. "Again school aid." Commonweal 84:489-90 Ag 5 '66.
3. "Aid to education." America 110:35-36 Ja 11 '64.
4. "Aid to education: a better deal." W. L. Miller. il Reporter 30: 20-3 Ap 23 '64.
5. "Aid to education: Administration's bill." New Republic 152:9 Ap 17 '65.
6. "Aid for the rich; impacted aid." il Newsweek 75:55 F 9, '70.
7. "Aid to education: planning is the key; excerpts from testimony before the House committee on eduation and labor," March 17, 1967: ed. by R. H. Smith. K. W. Lund, Pub W 191:40 Mr 27, '67.
8. "Aid to schools; what the President wants," US News 58:35 Ja 18 '65.
9. "Aiding the schools. Commweal 81:499-500, Ja 15 '65.
10. "Ambitious program for the 88th Congress." H. G. Sackett, NEA J 52:32 F '63.
11. "American council on education: conference designed to illuminate the ins and outs of grantsmanship." J. Walsh, Science 140:1383 Je 28 '63.

12. "Area vocational schools." M. Russo, Am Ed, 2:15-19 Je '66.

13. "Ax for the South: cutting off Federal funds from segregated schools." Time 88:32 D 16 '66.

14. "Best title of all; impact of Title II of the Elementary and secondary eduation act." D. Dempsey, Sat R 49:50 O 1 '66; Reply, D. Lacy, 49:26 O 29 '66.

15. "Beyond the school question." J. O'Gara. Commonweal 78:15 Mr 29 '63.

16. "Big federal move into eduation; Time essay." Time 85:44-5 Ap 30 '65.

17. "Biggest push yet for school integration; threat to cut off aid." US News 58:50-1 Mr 1 '65.

18. "Bill for education." New Repub 148:6-7 Je 15 '63.

19. "Billions for schools; who gets them." US News 61:48 O 31 '66.

20. "Broader federal support of schools." Sch & Soc 96:264+ Sub '68.

21. "Candor needed on federal aid to education." Chirstian Cent 81:1484 D 2 '64.

22. "Categorical aid." America 111:9 Jl 4 '64.

23. "Children as hostages? question of aid to impacted districts." Time 95:23 Ap 13 '70.

24. "Congress: a broad expansion of National defense education act passes relatively unnoticed. J. Walsh, Science 146:383-4 O 16 '64.

25. "Congress and school construction." H.C.F. Arnold, Arch Rec 135:18 F '64.

26. "Congress votes expanded aid to education measures." Pub W 190:54-5 O 31 '66.

27. "Crack in the ice; NEA resolutions on Federal support for public education." America 109:127 Ag 10 '63.

28. "Curse of crash education." R. C. Orem Nations Bsns 57:60-2+ Ag '69.

29. "Cut-off in Boston; concerning withholding federal funds." J. S. Doyle. New Repub 155:10 Ag 27 '66.

30. "Dilemma of federal aid." Time 81:84+ Ap 12 '63.

31. "Disadvantage of being poor; misuse of Title I funds." Nation 209:590 D 1 '69.

32. "Disbursement of federal aid by the Office of education, 1962-63." R. M. Walker, Sch Life, 46:15 Mr '64.

33. "Education act of 1965 introduced and debated" Library J 90:1486+ Mr. 15 '65.

34. "Education: a show of power over funds for innovation; ESEA money." R. Karp, Science 167:1709-11 Mr 27 '70.

35. "Education bill." Time 85:19 Ja 22 '65.

36. "Education bill amendments." America 112:275 F 27 '65.

37. "Education's billion-dollar baby; Elementary and secondary education act of 1965." E. B. Drew Atlan 218:37, 43 Jl '66.

38. "Education: case for federal aid, comprehensive planning discussed as costs and enrollment rise." J. Walsh, Science, 147:30-2 Ja 1 '65.

39. "Education funs and Title I of ESEA." C. B. Grannis, Pub W 197:42 Ja 12 '70.

40. "Education funds voted: who gets the money and how." US News 55:6 D 23 '63.

41. "Education in State of Union message; President's budget message." NEA J 52:4 F '63.

42. "Education message: can we believe it?" R. H. Smith Pub W 193:48 F 12 '68.

43. "Education special revenue sharing proposal; Commissioner's conferences held by USOE." G. Krettek and E. D. Cooke. Am Lb 2:380-1 Ap '71.

44. "Education stalemate." C. Jencks, New Repub 148:6 F 9 '63.

45. "Education: the revolution which never stops: address, October 8 1967." L. B. Jo;nson, Dept State Bul 57:569-71 O 30 '67.

46. "Education vouchers." P. A. Janssen, Am Ed 6:9-11 D '70.

47. "Education vouchers." C. Jancks, New Repub 163:19-21 Jl 4 '70.

48. "Education: weapon against poverty; economic opportunity act of 1964." Sch Life 47:23-24 O '64.

49. "Education: what next?" C. Jancks, New Repub 153:21-3 O 16 '65.

50. "Education wins another round." G. Krettek and E. D. Cooke, ALA Bul 63:1536 D '69.

51. "Elementary and secondary education act of 1965." ALA Bul 59:184-5 Mr '65.

52. "Elementary and secondary education amendments of 1969." J. S. Frohlicher Am Ed 6:7-9 Jl '70.

53. "ESEA amendments of 1966." G. Krettek and E. D. Cooke, ALA Bul 60:417-18 My '66.

54. "Federal aid and higher education." G. E. Snavely, Sch & Soc 91:86-8 F 23 '63.

55. "Federal aid and judicial review." Christian Cent 82:451-2 Ap 14 '65.

56. "Federal aid at last." America 112:602 Ap 24 '65.

57. "Federal aid bill." America 108:819 Je 8 '63.

58. "Federal aid controversy." America 111:204 Ag 29 '64.

59. "Federal aid, 1963." America 108:190 F 9 '63.

60. "Federal aid to education prospects improve." Christian Cent 82:231 F 24 '65.

61. "Federal aid vs. poverty." Sch & Soc 95:250 Ap 15 '67.

62. "Federal aid? will there be government control? and to whom will federal funds be paid?" J. M. Hanlon, America 110:418-19 Mr 28 '64.

63. "Federal challenge and peril to the American school; adaptation of address." December 17, 1965, F. M. Cordasco, Sch & Soc 94:263-5 Sum '66.

64. "Federal commitment to education; aid to schools and libraries." C. B. Grannis Pub W 190:69 Ag 1 '66.

65. "Federal funds." Am Ed 7:28-9 D '71.

66. "Federal funds (cont of) Federal money for education." Am Ed 3:22 Ap 26-7 my; 30-1 Je '67.

67. "Federal funds for education." Sat R 46:81 F 16 '63.

68. "Federal hand on local schools?" With interview by B. C. Willis, US News 59:54-9 N 8 '65.

69. "Federal influence distorts education: US programs create imbalance in colleges." Nations Bsns 51:31-3+ Mr '63.

70. "Federal influences on the future of American education." F. Parker, Sch & Soc 95:383-7 O 28 '67.

71. "Federal responsibility in education." America 116:674 My 6 '67.

72. "Federal school aid." R. Moley, Newsweek 65:100 F 22; 96 Mr 8 '65.

73. "Fight over federal aid to schools." Changing T 19:43-6 F '65.

74. "Figures on federal aid: Federal funds and school revenue." Sch & Soc 94:174 Ap 1 '66.

75. "First work of these times; analysis of the Elementary and secondary education act of 1965. Am Ed 1:13-20 Ap '65.
76. "Follow up: bill to continue Elementary and secondary education act (ESEA)" W. D. Boutwell, PTA Mag 64:11 Je '70.
77. "Fortune favors the informed, conderning the Elementary and secondary education act of 1965." America 112:700 My 15 '65.
78. "$4.6 billion baby; President Kennedy's
79. "Free choice; a voucher plan; giving all students the choice of attending either a public or a private school in California." R. Kirk, Nat R 21:598 Je 17 '69.
80. "Freedom of choice; suspending federal aid to southern districts." Newsweek 73:31 F 17 '69.
81. "Funds for school aid, a veto and then. . ." US News 68:4 F 9 '70.
82. "Going up fast: Office of education, budget to be doubled." Time 85:50 Ja 15 '65.
83. "Government and the schools." J. Justman, Sch & Soc 95:75-8 F 4 '67.
84. "Government's interest in education: Elementary and secondary education act of 1965; summary of address." Pub W 188:68-70+ D 6 '65.
85. "Government's plan to desegregate the suburbs." US News 61:76-8 O 10 '66.
86. "Grant programs for fiscal 1966: with list of programs." G. O. Dane, Am Ed 1:5-9.
87. "House reaffirms education priority." G. Krettek and E. D. Cooke, ALA Bul 63:1069-71 S '69.
88. "Hundred day mark; school-aid bill passed." Newsweek 65:26 Ap 19 '65.
89. "Impacted aid." W. D. Boutwell, PTA Mag 64:13 Mr '70.
90. "Impacted ghetto." D. Blackburn, Nation 210:51 My 4 '70.
91. "Impasse ended; Elementary and secondary education act of 1965." D. M. Kelley, Christian Cent 83:627-30 My 11 '66.
92. "Inequities of school finance." A. K. Campbell, Sat R 52:44+ Ja 11 '69.
93. "Inflation showdown over school funds." US News 68:6 F 2 '70.
94. "Is federal aid helping to end neighborhood schools?" US News 61:49-50 S 5 '66.
95. "Jencks tuition voucher plan." America 122:644-5 Je 20 '70.
96. "Johnson Juggernaut; school-aid bill passed with amendments." Time 89:12-12 Je 2 '67.
97. "Keppel speaks out on education bill; excerpts from interview." F. Keppel, Sr. School 86:1T F 19 '65.
98. "Landmark: major new program of Federal aid to education." Newsweek 62:71 D 23 '63.
99. "LBJ proposal: more aid for schools." US News 60:16 Mr 14 '66.
100. "Misuse of Title I." W. Roberts, Sat R. 52:2:65 D 20 '69.
101. "More federal aid for public schools." Pub W 195:38 Je 9 '69.
102. "New crackdown on local schools." US News 60:25-7 My 2 '66.
103. "New dimension; progress under Title III of the Elementary and secondary education act of 1965." H. L. Phillips Am Ed 2:15-20 Ap '66.
104. "New tack on School aid." America 124:111-12 F 6 '71.
105. "Next steps in federal aid." R. H. Wyatt, NEA J 53:35-6 Mr '64.
106. "1967 report on federal money and recent legislation for education." Am Ed 3:13-25 F '67.

107. "Nixon administration gives firm support to ESEA." S. Wagner, Pub W 195:34-5 Mr 24 '69.

108. "Nixon reviews mandatory education funds." Library J 95:3583 0 15 '70.

109. "No magic in vouchers." Nation 210:773 Je 29 '70.

110. "Non-compliance with desegregation guidelines." Sch & Soc 94:310+ 0 15 '66.

111. "One big gulp; twenty-four part federal aid bill. Time 81:49 F 8 '63.

112. "Pay as you go schooling; voucher plan." Newsweek 76:49 Ag 10n'70.

113. "Poor children; Washington research project and the NAACP legal defense fund report charges misuse of Title I funds." New Repub 161:9-11 N 22 '69.

114. "Poor education; Urban education task force report." New Repub 162:9-10 Mr 21 '70.

115. "Poor pay the price; cuts in funds." B.B. Stretch, Sat R 51:54 Jl 20 '68.

116. "Pound of cure for educational problems." B.J. Paschal, Sch & Soc 95:53-5 Ja 21 '67.

117. "Poverty war program with too much money." US News 62:15 Ap 17 '67.

118. "President Johnson speaks out on education; special statement for the National education association." L.B. Johnson, NEA J 53:12-14, Ja 64.

119. "President Kennedy and education." W.W. Brickman, Sch & Soc 92:93 Mr 7 '64.

120. "President Johnson's educational program for all children." W.W. Brickman, Sch & Soc 93:288 Sum '65.

121. "President's message on education; excerpts." L.B. Johnson Wilson Lib Bul 39:440+ F '65.

122. "President's new ideas, and a look at the expense." US News 62:104-5 Mr 13 '67.

123. "Price of hope offered and then denied; curtailing or eliminating educational and social programs." R.H. Smith, Pub W 192:38 Jl 31 '67.

124. "Promises fulfilled; progress under Title I of the Elementary and secondary education act of 1965. R. Goff Am Ed 2:10-17 F '66.

125. "Public higher education and the needs of government; excerpt from address." April 29, 1964, J.K. Pollock, Sch & Soc 92:45-7 F 8 '64.

126. "Public schools need federal aid." Christian Cent 81:390 Mr 25 '64.

127. "Reckoning postponed; orders to cut off federal aid to segregated Dixie school districts." Newsweek, 73:21-2 F 10 '69.

128. "Repackaging Federal Aid." Time 97:66-7 Ap 19 '71.

129. "Revenue sharing and your schools." W.D. Boutwell PTA Mag 65:15-16 Ap '71.

130. "Rush for the finish line seen under ESEA programs; summary of ABPC-ATPI meeting." Pub W 189:58-60 F 7 '66.

131. "School aid makes it at last." Bsns W p32 Ag 24 '63.

132. "More federal aid for cities?" US News 59:88 Ag 9 '65.

133. "Schools cry for more federal aid." Bsns W p56-8 O 9 '71.

134. "Shaping educational policy." D. Wolfe. Science 146:1117 N 27 '64.

135. "Shared services and conscience; purpose of the Elementary and secondary education act of 1965." America 114:542-3 Ap 16 '66.

136. "Shift in opinion; Gallup poll." America 108:245 F 23 '63.

137. "Some unsolved problems of federal aid to education." L.P. Minear, Sch & Soc 96:135-7 Mr 2 '68.

138. "South's schools; still under fire." us News 66:10 F 24 '69.
139. "Speaking out; why we need more federal aid for our schools." S McMurrin Sat Eve Post 236:6+ Mr 23 '63.
140. "Strength where it counts; progress under Title V of the Elementary and Secondary education act of 1965. R.L. Hopper. AM Ed 2:20-1 Je '66.
141. "Thrust and counterthrust in education policy making." R.F. Campbell and D.H. Layton, Ed Digest 33:4-7, Ap '68.
142. "Trouble with vouchers." M.R. Berube, Commonweal 93:14-17 Ja 29 '71.
143. "Title III of ESEA offers encouragement for innovation." N. Estes, NEA J 55:30-2, D '66.
144. "Voucher Plan debate: OEO funding experimental Jencks plan.." G. Elford America 126:87-91 Ja 29 '72.
145. "Voucher plan; NEA position." Todays Ed 59:80 N '70.
146. "What are Americans receiving in return for their heavy investment in education? excerpts of testimony." J Gardner; H. Howe, 2d, Am Ed 2:24-6 N '66.
147. "What Congress did to federal aid." W.D. Boutwell, PTA Mag 62:25 F '68.
148. "What Nixon won in a school bill; extension of the Elementary and secondary education act." US News 66:14 My 5 '69.
149. "White House plan for education; changes, cutbacks." US News 68:14-6 Ja 26 '70.
150. "Who pulled the teeth from Title VI?" G.W. Foster, jr Sat R 49:88 Ap 16 '66.

SCHOOL FINANCE

151. "Ahead for big-city schools: penny-pinching and turmoil. US News 71:24-6+ S 13 '71.
152. "Bad way to pay for schools." Life 71:42 D 10 '71.
153. "California doctrine." A.E. Wise Sat R 54:78-9+ N 20 '71.
154. "California scraps its school tax system." Bsns W p59-60 S 4 '71.
155. "Coming change in the property; with editorial comment." Bsns W p50-4+, 76, F 12 '72.
156. "Crisis in school finance." J.S. Berke, Ed Digest, 37:5-8 N '71.
157. "Dividing the cake; California Supreme court decision." Time 98:47 S 13 '71.
158. "Education's rigged lottery; address." October 12 1971, S.P. Marland, jr, Vital Speeches 38:122-5 D 1 '71.
159. "Exit the property tax? California Supreme court decision." Newsweek 78:61 S 13 '71.
160. "Financial crisis for public schools." US News 71:48-50 N 8 '71.
161. "Fresh blow against financing schools with property taxes." US News 72:66 Ja 10 '72.
162. "Getting the point; increase in school taxes passed." Youngstown, Ohio. Newsweek 73:65 My 19 '69.
163. "Growing protest against school costs." US News 67:36-7 O 20 '69.
164. "Illinois probes the state aid question; direct aid to parents program; with editorial comment." D. Suton, America 126:82-3, 84-7 Ja 29 '72.

165. "New financing for schools." America 125:363 N 6 '71.
166. "New financing tool." E. Edelman, Am Ed 5:20 D '69.
167. "Paying for good schools." New Repub 165:5-6 D 11 '71.
168. "Paying for public education; California Supreme court decision." Nation 213:226 S 20 '71.
169. "Property tax is obsolete." H. Howe, 2nd. Educ Digest 37:1-4 Ja '72.
170. "Public schools feel the money pinch." W.R. Grant, Commonweal 90: 167+ Ap 25 '69.
171. "Property taxes inadequate, new school financing needed; summary of address," November 1968, W.J. Cohen. Sr Schol 93:Schol Teach 5 Ja 10 '69.
172. "Refining the public schools." America 126:165 F 19 '72.
173. "Schools go begging." Newsweek 77:98 $\pm$ Je 7 '71.
174. "School taxes; decision by the California Supreme court." New Repub 165:9-10 O 2 '71.
175. "Squeezing the schools." Time 98:72 $\pm$ O 4 '71.
176. "Taxing for education." I. Silver, Commonweal 95:466-8 F 18 '72.
177. "Taxing question." Newsweek 79:48 Ja 31 '72.
178. "Taxpayer revolt keeps on rolling." US News 66:81 My 19 '69.
179. "Taxpayers to the barricades." Time 96:50 O 12 '71.
180. "Toward equality in school finance; National educational finance project." R.L. Johns Am Ed 7:3-6, N '71.
181. "Why ghetto schools fail." H.M. Levin Sat R 53:68-9 $\pm$ Mr 21 '70.

EDUCATIONAL JOURNALS AND PERIODICALS

## Federal Aid to Education (1969)

1. "Federal aid to education; teacher opinion poll." NEA Research division. Todays Ed 58:8 Ja '69.
2. "Federal educational programs and minority groups." H.A. Glickstein, bibliog J Negro Ed 38:303-14 Sum '69.
3. "Fraud charges to be investigated; United States." K Beavan, Times Ed. Sup 2846:12 D 5 '69.
4. "In defense of the harmful monopoly; merits and limitations of the voucher plan." E.J. Fax and W.B. Levenson. Phi Delta Kappan 51:131-5 N '69.
5. "Make education America's choice. H.C. Ruark, jr. Ed Screen AV G 48:7 $\pm$ S '69.
6. "On looking gift horses in the mouth; the federal government and the schools." J.M. Atkin. Ed Forum 34:9-20 N '69.
7. "Performance proposals for educational funding; a new approach to federal resource allocation." l.m. Lessinger and D.H. Allen. Phi Delta Kappan 51:136-7 N '69.
8. "Sources and variations in federal support for education." A.R. Munse Am Ed 5:29 N '69.
9. "Toward a new fiscal federalism." M.I. Weidenbaum. Phi Dalta Kappan 51:154-7 N '69.

10. "Trends and musts in federal education legislation." F.D. Murnaghan, jr. and R. Mandel, Phi Delta Kappan 50:554-9 Je '69.
11. "What does a district do with Federal funds?" E. Nowicki and W.A. Schuier; T. Abraham, Pa Sch J 118:92-7+ D '69.
12. "Widespread misuse of title I funds blasted in private research report." W. Steif, Nations Sch 84:84+ D '69.

### (1970)

13. "Accountability." R.P. Krull, jr. Instr 79:16 F '70.
14. "Distribution of federal school aid funds; who wins? who loses?" J.W. Guthrie and S.B. Lawton. Ed Adm Q 6:47-62 Wint '70.
15. "Education for the 70's" W.C. Young Clear H 44:387-90 Mr '70.
16. "Federal aid to education: 1945-63 G.A. Kizer bibliog Hist Ed Q 10:84-102 Spr '70.
17. "Federal help is necessary." A Cranston, CTA J 66:17-18 Ja '70.
18. "Federal state partnership for education; fifth annual report, Advisory council on state departments of education." (OE 23050-70) US Office Ed Pub 1970:182p
19. "Grants are not made in heaven; generalized model for successful coordination of grants and funded projects." D.V. Silagyi, Col & Univ Bsns 49:45-53 O '70.
20. "Impact of federal programs on learning to read in Appalachia." B. Mynhier, Int Read Assn Conf Papers (Reading goals for the disadvantaged) 11:219-30 '70.
21. "Indirect costs of federally financed projects." W. Simmons, Am Sch & Univ 43:26+ O '70.
22. "New impact for the federal partner." J.E. Allen, Jr. Compact 3: 48-50 Al '69.
23. "New strings for title I: district must show comparability; interview" R.L. Fairley, Nations Sch 86:32-4 O '70.
24. "Roles of the states and federal government in metropolitan educational organization." M.M. Milstein. bibliog Urban Ed 5:179-98 Jl '70.
25. "School finance." bibliog Yrbk Sch Law 1970:153-203.
26. "Separate OE bill should speed '71 funds to schools." Nations Sch 86:66 Ag '70.

### (1970)

27. "Case for a new realignment of financial responsibilities for education." H.V. Webb, Am Sch. Bd J. 159:29-31 D '71.
28. "Competing for the federal dollar." H.A. Williams, jr. Compact 5:5-6 Ap '71.
29. "Estimated revenue receipts for elementary and secondary schools by governmental source, by state, 1969-70." Compact 5:35 Ap '71.
30. "Federal funds in education: when does use become abuse?" E. Green Educ Forum 36:7-20 N '71.
31. "Federal, local, and in between." J.M. Atkin, Assn Sup and Curric Develop Yrbk 1971:259-68.
32. "Fiasco in integration spending?" Nations Sch 87:20-1 Ja '71.

33. "Guide to OE-administered programs, fiscal year 1972." United States office of education, Amer Education 7:32-44 Ag '71.
34. "Highlights of O.E.'s 1972 budget." J.R. Ottino Am Educ 7:36 Ag '71.
35. "Is revenue sharing a new mirage." L.J. Stiles, J. Educ Res 65: inside cover S '71.

## State Aid to Education

36. "Boardmen aren't warmed much by state equalizing plans for education." Am Sch Bd J 157:9-11+ D '69.
37. "Conant plan for state financing of all public schools." W.P. McLure, Integ Ed 7:52-4 S '69.
38. "Conant state finance plan gets qualified approval; school administrators opinion poll; with comments by J.B. Conant." Nations Sch 83: 70-1 Ja '69.
39. "Judicial assault on state school aid laws; problems and prognosis." A.W. Steinhilber, Phi Delta Kappan 51:151-53 N '69.
40. "School finance." EMMcWherter, Ill Ed 57:249-52 F '69.
41. "State assumption of school costs." F. Bryant, Compact 3:38-40 Ag '69.
42. "State role in financing public schools." L.L. Ecker-Racz and E. McCloone, Ed Digest 34:5-8 D '68.
43. "Trends and issues in statewide coordination." C.H. White, bibliog Ed Rec 49:325-31 Sum '68.

## Education Vouchers

44. "Adam Smith rides again." K. Beavan, Times Ed Sup 2872:15 Je 5 '70.
45. "Boardmen can't think of one good thing to say about voucher plans." Am Sch Bd J 158:33-7 O '70.
46. "Education vouchers." P.A. Janssen, Am Ed 6:9-11 D '70.
47. "Education vouchers; peril or panacea? symposium." bibliog Teach Col Rec 72:327-404 F '71.
48. "Educational voucher plan. J.L. Carter, Am Biol Teach 33:2 Ja '71.
49. "Educational voucher plan. "R.W. MacNeven Sch & Com 57:30-1 N '70.
50. "Giving parents money for schooling; education vouchers." C Jencks, Phi Delta Kappan 52:49-52 S '70.
51. "Voucher system; bane or boon?" F.W. Hill Am Sch & Univ 42:16-17 Jl '70.

## Legal Periodicals

—"Community control of the public school—practical approach for achieving equal educational opportunity: A socio-legal perspective." Suffolk U.L Review 3:308 Spring '69.
—"Community control, public policy, and the limits of law." D.L. Kirp Mich L Rev 68:1355 Je '70.
—"Constitutional Law: financing public education under the equal protection clause." U Fla L Rev 23:590 Spring '71.

—"Constitutional law: Florida limitation on local property tax rate for education violates equal protection." Duke L J 1970:1033 O '70.

—"Cost of education and the federal income tax: B Wolfman. F.R.D 42:535 N '67.

—"Dilemma of federal impact area school aid." Minn L Rev 55:33 N '70.

—"Educational opportunity: a workable constitutional test for state financial structures." J.E. Coon, W.H. Clune, III, S.D. Sugarman. Calif L Rev 57:305 Ap '69.

—"Education vouchers." J. Areen, Harv. Civil Rights L Rev 6:466 My '71.

—"Educational vouchers—challenge to the wall of separation?" Valperaiso U. L Rev 5:569 Spring '71.

—"Elementary and Secondary education act of 1965: the birth of compensatory education." C.L. Lo Presti, Urban L Ann 1971:145 '71.

—"Equal educational opportunity: a case for the children." St. John's L Rev 46:280 D '71.

—"Equality of educational opportunity: judicial supervision of public education. N.J. Bloomfield, So Calif L Rev 43:275 '70.

—"Equal educational opportunity: the emerging role of the state board of education." L. Koten BU L Rev 50:211 Spring '70.

—"Equal educational opportunity: the limits of constitutional jurisprudence undefined." P.B. Kurland, U Chi L Rev 38:583 Summer '68.

—"Family choice in education: a model state system for vouchers." J.E. Coons, S.D. Sugarman, Calif L Rev 59:321 Mr '71.

—"Federal aid to education: Title I at the operational level." L and Soc Order 1971:321 '71.

—"Governmental aid to elementary and secondary education." Notre Dame Law 43:734 Je '68.

—"Intrastate inequalities in public education: the case of judicial relief under the equal protection clause." J. Silard, S. White, Wis L Rev 1970:7 '70.

—"National School Lunch Program." U Pa L Rev 119:372 D '70.

—"Notes on the educational opportunity bank." K. Shell Nat Tax J 23: 214 Je '70.

—"Pennsylvania's state aid to education formula: a goal of uniform equalized education." U Pitt L Rev 30:41 Fall '68.

—"Political economy of American public school legislation." G.G. West J L and Econ 10:101 O '67.

—"Proceedings of National tax association seminar on balancing our federal-state-local fiscal system." Nat Tax J 24:273 S '71.

—"Public aid to Private education." Catholic U. L Rev 20:528 Spring '71.

—"Racism and inferior Education." H.H. Punke Alabam Law 32:165 Ap 71.

—"Reflections on the implications of Title I of the elementary and secondary education act of 1965." R.F. Drinan, Catholic Law 15:179 Summer '69.

—"Reforming Title I-a study in grant design." A.L. Ginzberg, G.R. Wilensky, Nat. Tax J. 24:235 Je '71.

—"Religion, higher education and the constitution." P.G. Kauper, Alabama L Rev 19:275 Spring '67.

—"Serrano v Priest in Iowa: financing public education under the fourteenth amendment." Ia L Rev 57:378 D '71.